The Essence of
JEET KUNE DO

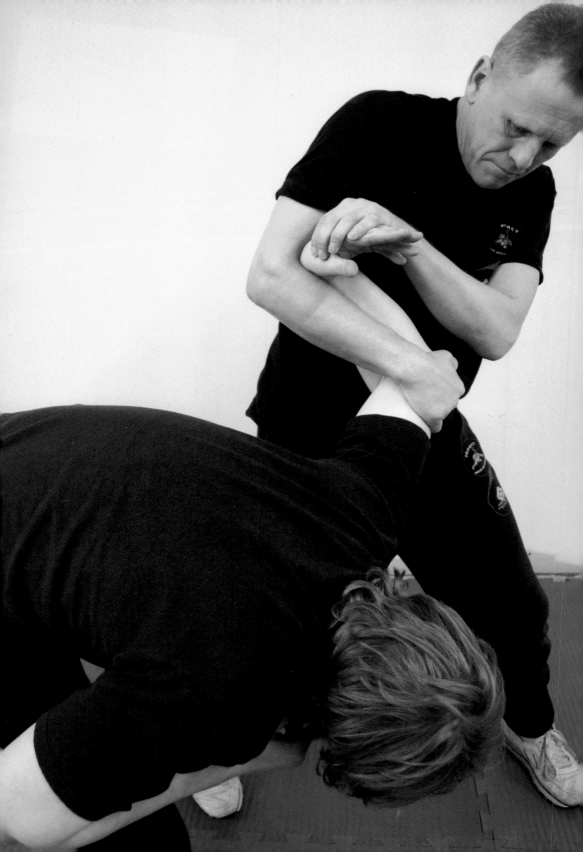

The Essence of JEET KUNE DO

Dave Carnell

To Mark,
"Thanks for training
with the Impact family."
All the Best
Sifu Dave

THE CROWOOD PRESS

First published in 2010 by
The Crowood Press Ltd
Ramsbury, Marlborough
Wiltshire SN8 2HR

www.crowood.com

British Library Cataloguing-in-Publication Data
A catalogue record for this book is available from the British Library.

ISBN 978 1 84797 220 0

Disclaimer
Please note that the author and the publisher of this book are not responsible
in any manner whatsoever for any damage or injury of any kind that may
result from practising, or applying, the principles, ideas, techniques and/or
following the instructions/information described in this publication. Since the
physical activities described in this book may be too strenuous in nature for
some readers to engage in safely, it is essential that a doctor be consulted
before undertaking training.

Designed and typeset by Focus Publishing,
11a St Botolph's Road, Sevenoaks, Kent TN13 3AJ

Printed and bound in China by Leo Paper Products Ltd

Contents

Foreword *by Cass Magda*

It is a great pleasure to see this companion to Dave Carnell's book, *Jeet Kune Do – A Core Structure Training Manual*, finally realized. In this latest book, the reader receives an in-depth understanding of the technical and philosophical roots of Jeet Kune Do. From there, progression is to the more advanced training concepts and progressions. The knowledge of Jeet Kune Do technique is one thing; the method to train them is another and that is where the essence of real JKD lies.

Knowing the methods of training and understanding the philosophies and attitudes behind those methods will give the reader the ability to personalize their own training in JKD and achieve their full potential.

Jeet Kune Do is known by many, but truly practised by few. Dave Carnell is one of the few.

Cass Magda
2010

Foreword *by Chris Kent*

I was immensely pleased when Dave Carnell asked me to write a foreword for his latest book. I first met Dave in 1984 while I was serving as Dan Inosanto's personal assistant when he was teaching JKD seminars in England. In the years that followed, Dave and I developed a friendship built upon commonality of desire and purpose; the perpetuation of the art and philosophy of Jeet Kune Do. I consider Dave Carnell to be one of the best and brightest Jeet Kune Do instructors in England, or the world for that matter. In his neverending quest to expand his knowledge and understanding with regard to JKD, he has trained extensively with many of the art's top instructors. In addition, he has conducted his own exhaustive research and investigation into all aspects of the art. A consummate martial art professional, sincerity, integrity and devotion to quality are hallmarks of Dave's teaching.

Jeet Kune Do is a single art, but the expressions of that art are many. This causes problems for those individuals who want everything laid out in nice, neat little packages. Even today, misconceptions concerning the art abound. To take a dynamic, fluid martial art training process such as Jeet Kune Do and convey it effectively in a one-dimensional medium, such as a book, is a difficult task, but Dave has succeeded in doing that. Building upon his first book, The Essence of Jeet Kune Do shares with the reader some of the philosophical principles which underpin the art and sheds light on many of the foundations or building blocks of Jeet Kune Do. There are chapters dealing with Wing Chun Gung Fu, Western boxing and Western fencing; combative arts from which Bruce Lee drew and absorbed many 'essences' such as tactile awareness, timing, distance and broken rhythm. In addition, there are chapters devoted to various combative tools that are an integral part of the JKD arsenal, as well as chapters on grappling skills and speed development. Finally there is a chapter on how to train with focus gloves.

The information that lies within the pages of this book will be of benefit to all JKD practitioners, or any martial artist for that matter. *The Essence of Jeet Kune Do* will help to make clear what Jeet Kune Do is truly about and provide the reader with the knowledge they need to increase both their understanding of the art and to enhance their personal performance.

Chris Kent
2010

Dedication

To the spirit of Sijo Bruce Lee

To Si-Gung Dan Inosanto who, 'when the going gets tough', inspires me to keep going.

To my Sifu, Cass Magda, who helped me hack away the unessential.

To all first, second and third generation Jeet Kune Do instructors who have helped me along the 'Martial Way'.

To the 'Carnell Clan', may they grow strong and healthy.

To my partner, Keely, for her continued support, patience and love.

Acknowledgements

My special thanks to Carol Woods who has given her time freely to proof-read and type the manuscript, and helped keep things on track; to Simon McGovern for his keen perception in his photographic skills and his creative art work; to my loyal students John Boote, Tom Wood, Steve Wan, Simon McGovern, Jon Hand, Mark Cotterill, Neal Haxton and my son Daniel Carnell for helping with the demonstrations in the photographs.

Fig. 1. Mark Cotterill, Steve Wan, John Boote, Dave Carnell, Tom Wood, Simon McGovern, Jon Hand and Neal Haxton.

Preface – About the Author

Dave Carnell began his training in martial arts at an early age, dabbling in judo with his friends. He returned to the martial arts as a teenager, inspired by the movies and television shows of the 1970s; this was when he saw his first glimpse of the impressive Bruce Lee. His first serious training was at the local Lau-Gar Kung Fu School and lasted approximately twelve months. Dave then started to train in a system called Chi-San-Tao – a blend of styles that included Wing Chun gung fu. He knew that this was the same art that Bruce Lee had gained his foundation in. With his interest in Wing Chun growing, Dave decided that it was this system that he would like to study in greater depth. He met and trained with many of the UK's top Wing Chun sifus of the time, including John Darwin, Danny Connor, Simon Lau and Samuel Kwok. Dave trained extensively with Samuel Kwok and was instrumental in the development and production of his book *Path to Wing Chun*, becoming one of the first instructors for the Samuel Kwok Martial Arts Association. Dave was in turn introduced to Samuel's teacher Ip Chun, the eldest son of Ip Man, who was Bruce Lee's Wing Chun teacher.

During this period, Dave was studying on a three-year college foundation course in art and design which was to lead to a degree. However, he never went on to do the degree, instead choosing to be a professional martial arts teacher and opening up his school full time. In 1984, whilst training and researching with various Wing Chun teachers, Dave came to realize that each sifu had their own individual interpretation of the art and he wanted to find out more about this idea of individual perspectives. During this time Dan Inosanto came to give a seminar in London, which Dave attended hoping to find another angle on the Wing Chun system. This was a turning point in his martial arts: it was a first-hand introduction to Jeet Kune Do and the many other arts that Guro Dan was into at the time. In his own words, Dave was just 'blown away'. His eyes were opened to the speed, skill and sophistication of not only Dan himself, but of his young assistants at that time, Cass Magda and Chris Kent.

After this first seminar, Dave continued to attend most of Inosanto's seminars, including those of his students Larry Hartsell, Chris Kent, Cass Magda and Tim Tackett. He also attended other first generation Bruce Lee students' seminars, including ones by Dan Lee, Ted Wong, Richard Bustillo and Jerry Poteet. This continued until Dave was inviting most of these people to do seminars in his own school, and was in return invited to train in the USA.

Dave continued to train on a private basis with Cass Magda. In 1990 he became authorized to teach JKD, Kali and Silat. During this time Dave became a JKD advisor and columnist for several years with *Martial Arts Illustrated* magazine, producing and compiling the book *What's in a Name – Jeet Kune Do* for MAI publications. Dave was also the technical advisor on the DVD *Bruce Lee – Martial Arts Master*, which led to him being introduced to many of Bruce Lee's friends and students from the USA. He spent many hours with them, compiling and cross-referencing material and training methods to get the full picture of Jeet Kune Do.

Over many years of training, Dave has become a senior instructor for Cass Magda's MI Association and supervising instructor for the UK, with branches throughout the country. As director of the Impact Martial Arts Academy, he is now a sought-after instructor on the seminar circuit, teaching throughout the UK and across Europe and America. Dave was the first person to take Jeet Kune Do to Poland, appearing on prime time television to demonstrate the art.

In 2007 Dave was recommended to The Crowood Press to write their first Jeet Kune Do book. *Jeet Kune Do – A Core Structure Training Manual* was published in 2008 and quickly became a bestseller with great reviews, which led to this companion book, *The Essence of Jeet Kune Do*.

With his 'beginner's mind' approach, Dave still continues to train and learn new aspects of the martial arts, his current interest being the ground game. His most recent achievements include being awarded his brown belt 2nd tab in Gracie Barra Brazilian jiu jitsu and his graduation from the Magda Institute, California, USA.

Introduction

Welcome to *The Essence of Jeet Kune Do*. Although this book can stand alone, it is best used as a companion volume to *Jeet Kune Do – A Core Structure Training Manual* (also published by Crowood), as many areas should be cross-referenced.

My first idea was to write a manual of advanced techniques and in many respects the material in this book would be considered advanced, but Jeet Kune Do is all about mastery of the basics – a few simple things refined and honed to perfection – and so advanced training requires constant maintenance of the basic core structure.

I came across the eventual theme for this book while reading through Bruce Lee's personal notes. In his studies, Lee would write questions to himself regarding the existing styles of martial arts that he was exposed to. He would ask 'How do I draw the essence and make it work for me?', meaning not the styles themselves, but their qualities such as attitude, economy, good form, speed, power and so on. He listed the pros and cons of various arts, wanting to know their strengths and weaknesses so that he might integrate the strengths and exploit the weaknesses. From this came the question to myself and the idea for this book, 'What are the defining essences of Jeet Kune Do?'

Fortunately, Bruce Lee left many clues along the way. He was an avid notemaker, writing down all of his training routines and cataloguing his research methodically. In a letter to a friend he said, 'I'm having a Gung Fu system drawn up. This system is a continuation of chiefly Wing Chun, boxing and fencing.' Although Lee later came to believe that there should be no fixed method of fighting, he firmly believed there was a progressive way to train. In Defining the Essence of Jeet Kune Do, I have tried to capture some of the progression of the art. This is a difficult thing to achieve. To write about and put into pictures an art that is alive and forever moving is not an easy task. While this is not intended as an instruction manual, certain techniques are shown in order to express various principles of the art, but remember that the examples are just that, examples and are not the only way. Included in this book are the three core arts of Wing Chun, boxing and fencing. Ask any Jeet Kune Do instructor about these arts and most give a simple answer: 'Wing Chun – sensitivity; boxing – the tools; fencing – footwork'. However, the true answer lies much deeper and hopefully after reading this book the reader will have a much greater understanding of the roots and true development of Jeet Kune Do.

Inside, you will find a breakdown of the centre line theory, the mechanics to develop power and speed, advanced footwork and the tactics for fighting that were developed by Bruce Lee and are still relevant today. There are more tools, including various hand strikes, elbows, knees, head butts and advanced kicks. Lee said that the whole body should be used as a weapon and that we should employ any means possible to get the job done.

If Jeet Kune Do is about being well rounded in all ranges of combat, then no slice of the pie can be left out. There is a saying that '90 per cent of all fights end up on the ground'. It is therefore important to have the grappling game covered and so you will find a chapter dedicated to both stand-up grappling and escape from the ground, either by getting back to your feet or reversing a bad position to a more superior one where you can strike or break something. Although at the time of his death Bruce Lee was researching grappling, it was the weakest link in the chain, so I feel it is important for the Jeet Kune Do practitioner to continue the journey and keep up with the current trends in the martial arts.

A chapter has been given to focus gloves – these simple padded hand mitts are the most valuable piece of training equipment available to the Jeet Kune Do practitioner and should be exploited to the highest degree.

As noted above, Lee researched the pros and cons of the arts available in his day and looked for ways to draw out the essence and strengths of each. If Jeet Kune Do is to remain at the cutting edge of the martial arts, it is important to continue this research in order to fit in with any opponent. The key to this is to train like an athlete, be in the best shape possible and be well rounded in all ranges of combat. I hope Defining the Essence of Jeet Kune Do helps both to expand and deepen a practitioner's understanding and development in the art and philosophy of Jeet Kune Do.

1 The Philosophy of Jeet Kune Do – Its Origin and Development

The fighting art of Bruce Lee is deeply entrenched in the philosophies of Taoism, Zen and the works of Krishnamurti. As a child, Bruce was introduced by his father to Tai Chi Chuan, the Chinese 'internal' martial art practised for health and self-defence, and so was exposed to its underlying Taoist concepts. From the age of thirteen, Bruce studied Wing Chun Gung Fu under the legendary Grandmaster Yip Man, who also directed Lee towards the philosophy of Lao Tzu and the interplay of movement through the Yin–Yang, the seemingly opposite forces of hard and soft that actually complement each other.

During Lee's training with Yip Man he would find himself sometimes becoming tense in both body and mind. Yip Man advised Lee to relax, to become calm and to learn the 'art of detachment'. In the effort of trying to relax, Lee found himself becoming even more tense. Yip Man further advised Lee to try to flow with the natural bend of things. In the end, Yip Man told Bruce to take a week off school to ponder and absorb his words. During this week alone, Lee continued to practise and meditate on Yip Man's words, but to no avail. Later, giving up, he decided to go down to the harbour and take a boat trip. While lost in thought he became angry with himself and struck out at the water, to no effect. He struck again and again until a realization came upon him. He tried to grab the water and it simply trickled out of his hand. This was it, the true essence of Gung Fu, 'to be like water'. It has no shape or form, so it can become all forms. It is the softest substance that can penetrate the hardest. Water can crash, destroying everything in its path; it can adapt and change its course without thought or seep through the tiniest crack. This was what he needed to be like – the 'nature of water'. At that moment, the reflection of a seagull on the water caught his eye and, as he followed the bird's reflection as it flew above, the words of Yip Man floated back to him – 'learn the art of detachment'. At last he had his answer. When facing an opponent his thoughts and emotions, should pass like the reflection of the bird on the water. He must let go of them, so that there are no blockages or interference of the conscious mind, to be in a state of Wu-Hsin, 'no-mindedness', and let the techniques flow through his body following their own course like the nature of water. To be in a state of 'non-doing', or Wu-Wei, was to trust the techniques to work. Forgetting about himself and fitting in with his opponent was to have spontaneous action.

In 1961 Lee enrolled at the University of Washington, majoring in Philosophy (Lee was an American citizen, having been born when his actor father's troupe was touring the States in 1940). He spent most of his spare time immersed in the Chinese Philosophy section of the library, always relating what he learnt to his art of Gung Fu. He came to believe that the Gung Fu idea of hard and soft styles was wrong and did not follow the Taoist ideas of formlessness and being in harmony with an opponent. He came to believe that hard and soft could not be separated, but should be one continual interplay of movement, Yin and Yang. Without resisting or striving, one yields (Yin energy) against an opponent's force (Yang energy). When the opponent's force goes to the extreme, it returns to Yin energy. In this moment of softness, one attacks with Yang energy. This was the nature of fitting in with an opponent, to harmonize rather than oppose force with force. Lee called his new martial art Non-Classical Gung Fu and set up a series of schools to teach it.

In January 1965 a Chinese delegation demanded that Bruce stop teaching Gung Fu to non-Chinese, or they would be forced to close his school down by way of a challenge match against a Gung Fu master named Wong Jak Man. Bruce took up the challenge, but although he won he was tired and out of breath. He concluded that his adherence to a particular style of fighting had led to the match lasting longer than he thought it should have. From this encounter he later realized that the notion of styles came into conflict with his Taoist beliefs of fitting in with an opponent. He had relentlessly stuck to the Wing Chun pattern of chain punching and had tired himself out. Caged inside a style of attack, he had limited his ability to fit in with his opponent.

Over time, Lee re-evaluated his training methods. He started to develop a more athletic way of training based on conditioning and fitness, with a strong emphasis on intercepting an opponent's attack. His idea was to stop-hit an opponent during his attack or, better still, to intercept him on his preparation to attack. Lee chose the name

Jeet Kune Do, or Way of the Intercepting Fist, to describe his new art – the defining principle being that of interception.

Along with the new name, Lee introduced a new emblem for his art. It consisted of the symbol Yin–Yang with two arrows moving around it. The arrows emphasized the interdependence of all things in an unceasing interplay of movement. Lee also added the Chinese characters, 'having no way as way, having no limitation as limitation', which became his motto. Fitting in with an opponent's movement and not being boxed in by a particular style or method allowed for freedom of self-expression.

In 1970 Lee sustained a serious back injury during weight training, which led to him needing bed rest for six months. Unable to train or teach, he began to focus even more on the underpinning philosophy of his art. As well as compiling seven volumes of notes on the physical aspects of fighting, Lee also delved deeply into reading and reflecting on the works of great philosophers, becoming, in particular, an avid reader of Krishnamurti. What Krishnamurti believed about organized religion paralleled what Bruce thought about organized martial art styles. They both felt that the truth was outside of all set patterns and was to be felt in the moment of everyday living. To free oneself from all imposed restrictions was the way, whether it be restrictions of religious dogma or restrictions of martial art styles.

A few years later, Lee came to the realization that even the name Jeet Kune Do was contrary to his philosophy. The Way of Intercepting was only one aspect of his beliefs and to base his system on one aspect alone was to leave out all others, as the name suggests. Lee came to realize also that where there is a way, there are limitations and these are the traps that squeeze freedom of expression.

In his final years, Lee felt that to fuss over the name Jeet Kune Do was to focus on the name and not what the art could do for the individual. He said that if you say it is different from this or from that, you have missed the point of the underpinning philosophy. He moved away from an art based on the way of interception to the conceptual idea of 'the way of no way'. Around this time he closed the LA China Town school, as he had come to the same belief as Krishnamurti – that the truth is outside of all organizations, systems and methods and he did not want his students to follow his way as way, but to find the truth for themselves.

Lee went on to share his art and philosophy through the media of film up until the time of his death and examples of his philosophy abound in his later movies. The more control he gained over the production of the movies, the more chance he had to drop in subtle nuggets of wisdom, the most famous being the early opening scenes of *Enter the Dragon*.

Through the journey of Lee's life one comes to see that his philosophy became an extension of his martial art, a true embodiment of the Yin–Yang principle. It is important that Lee's knowledge and experiences are preserved, but equally important that we remember that it is Lee's knowledge and experience and not our own. Bruce Lee was a pointer to the truth and not the truth itself, although it is possible to use Lee's work as a foundation from which to develop and grow and discover the truth for ourselves.

2 Wing Chun – At the Core of Jeet Kune Do

Wing Chun Gung Fu was the original art that Bruce Lee trained in before leaving Hong Kong to start his new life in the United States. Although he never completed this system, he trained long and hard enough to programme the neurological pathways required to make its principles work for him. While in Hong Kong, Bruce Lee was taught Wing Chun Gung Fu by Wong Shun Leung under the watchful eye of Grandmaster Yip Man, and he often trained with senior student William Cheung. Even back then Bruce wanted to be the best practitioner in the clan and he often asked how he could beat certain members of the school, including his friend William Cheung and even his teacher Wong Shun Leung. This competitive nature led Wong Shun Leung to worry about Bruce and he told him that he should have only one opponent – himself. When Lee left for the United States, Wong Shun Leung warned him to watch out for Western boxers.

On his arrival in the US, Bruce was soon training with a small group of friends, which included talented judo players, boxers and street fighters. It didn't take long for Lee to start making adjustments to his existing style. These changes came about for various reasons, one of them being that Westerners were mostly much bigger and stronger than him. He was also still driven to try to become the best fighter in the Wing Chun clan. After returning to Hong Kong on two separate occasions, Bruce realized that no matter how hard he trained in the US his seniors in Hong Kong were also training and improving, so to beat them he would have to look outside the Wing Chun principles. He started to experiment by adjusting the angles and stance of Wing Chun Gung Fu. These developments he later called Jun Fan Gung Fu. This was the martial art that he taught at his schools in Seattle and later in the early days of his Oakland, California, school.

Once into the development of his Jeet Kune Do, Bruce looked back and made the observation that although he owed his present achievement to his previous training in Wing Chun Gung Fu, his present method of fighting was far more alive and efficient. This new system was stripped of all wasted motion and elongated swinging movements. Its economical structure was designed for directness, with a strong emphasis on sensitivity and tactile awareness. Many of the principles of Wing Chun were retained in Jeet Kune Do and some were modified along the way. The obvious things kept in Jeet Kune Do were the naming of certain hand positions, for example pak-sau, lop-sau, fook-sau, huen-sau, jau-sau and jut-sau (all covered in *Jeet Kune Do – A Core Structure Training Manual* by Dave Carnell). The bong-sau and the tan-sau hand positions were relegated to the sensitivity exercises that were still practised in Jeet Kune Do, but were given more of a back seat in the LA period of Lee's development. Chi-sau sensitivity training had given Lee really strong defence on close range but did not completely eliminate the possibility of being hit by a good boxer. Moving to long range non-attachment outside of an opponent's hitting range and having the ability to close the gap extremely fast solved this problem.

The principal elements of Wing Chun Gung Fu are discussed below.

The Immovable Elbow

The key to the Wing Chun defence is the immovable elbow theory. This allows the arms to move in any direction while the elbow remains in the same space. The lead arm is held out in front and is known as the man-sau (inquisitive hand). This arm acts as an antenna and is the first line of defence against an incoming attack. The rear hand is known as the whu-sau (guard hand) and is held at the rear in front of the chest. The hands are positioned in such a way as to allow them both to attack and defend simultaneously. This is known as lin-sil-die-dar (see Figs 2 and 3).

In Wing Chun Gung Fu this is called 'defending the four gates'. Lee's modifications to the immovable elbow theory led to Jeet Kune Do's four-corner defence (see *Jeet Kune Do – A Core Structure Training Manual*). Keeping within the four-corner structure is to abide by the principles of 'economy of movement', using just enough movement to clear the line of the opponent's attack.

Fig. 2. Front view of the Wing Chun bai-jong.   Fig. 3. Side view of the Wing Chun bai-jong.

The Centre Line Theory

The underlying thread of Wing Chun's centre line theory runs throughout Jeet Kune Do. The theory is broken down into three parts, the mother line, the self centre line and the central plane.

The Mother Line The mother line is a line that runs from the top of the head down through the body to the ground and forms the central axis of rotation for the Wing Chun man. When the body pivots in rotation, the central axis does not move (see Diagram 1).

Lee recognized the limitations of the mother line and by freeing himself from this structure it allowed him to shift and angulate the upper body to accommodate more punching angles and lines of attack.

The Self Centre Line The self centre line is a line that runs vertically down the surface of the body, dividing it into two equal parts.

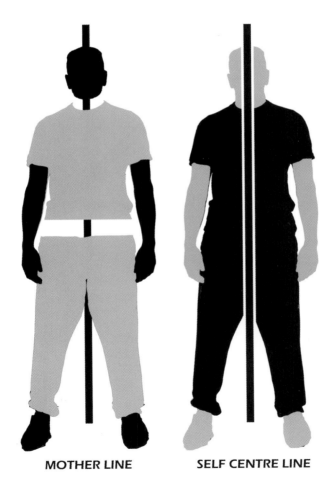

MOTHER LINE   **SELF CENTRE LINE**

Diagram 1. The mother line and the self centre line.

Most of the vital organs of the body lie close to this line, so it is important for the Wing Chun man to protect this line and to focus his attack on an opponent's self centre line (see Diagram 1).

In Jeet Kune Do's on-guard stance the hands are still positioned to protect the self centre line.

The Centre Line Plane   The centre line plane radiates out from the Wing Chun man's mother line and connects to that of an opponent's mother line. This is somewhat like the turret of a tank pivoting so that the barrel faces an opponent while the opponent is facing away. This is known as centre line advantage (see Diagram 2 and Fig. 4).

Diagram 2. The centre line plane.

Fig. 4. Centre line plane advantage.

The Cutting Angle

In Wing Chun Gung Fu a 45-degree angle is used to deflect incoming blows. Rather than using force against force, the 45-degree angle allows the blow to slide by, or the blow can be shut down using the same structure. For example, bong-sau, wing arm deflects the strike, while pak-sau shuts down the blow (see Fig 5).

Both the bong and the pak use the 45-degree cutting angle. This structure was retained in Jeet Kune Do and although the angles of the arms have been modified they still allow for the cutting angle to be applied. This became known as the wedge principle. If you imagine two triangles colliding head on, one or the other will be deflected off the centre line plane (see Diagram 3). Now imagine one of the triangles cutting in ahead on the 45-degree angle.

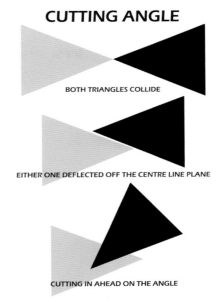

CUTTING ANGLE

BOTH TRIANGLES COLLIDE

EITHER ONE DEFLECTED OFF THE CENTRE LINE PLANE

CUTTING IN AHEAD ON THE ANGLE

Diagram 3. The cutting angle breakdown.

Fig. 5. The cutting angle of the pak-sau shuts an opponent down.

This 45-degree angle excludes the opposing triangle by deflecting or jamming it. This structure was the key to Jeet Kune Do's hand immobilization attack and its interception with timed hits (see *Jeet Kune Do – A Core Structure Training Manual*).

The Transverse Abdominis

Although Lee changed the classical Wing Chun stance to something resembling more of the Western boxing stance, as this allowed for greater mobility, one of the key Wing Chun postural positions was hidden in Jeet Kune Do's on-guard stance. In the Wing Chun's yee gee kim yeung ma basic training stance, the hips are thrust forward and the tail bone tucked in, engaging the transverse abdominis muscle (see Figs 6–7).

When engaged, this muscle acts like the tightening of a belt that stabilizes the pelvis and supports the torso. This core stability is

 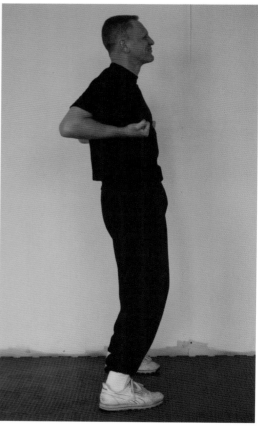

Fig. 6. Front view of the Wing Chun yee gee kim yeung ma stance.

Fig. 7. Side view of the Wing Chun yee gee kim yeung ma stance.

transferred into the Jeet Kune Do on-guard stance. By engaging the tranverse abdominis the centre of gravity is pulled slightly forward, which helps with all explosive movement (see Figs 8–9).

To the casual onlooker, the later stages of Jeet Kune Do do not physically resemble the traditional Wing Chun Gung Fu, but with further investigation one can find many of the underlying principles of Wing Chun deeply embedded in its structure. So Wing Chun is truly at the core of Jeet Kune Do.

Fig. 8. Wing Chun front stance engaging the transverse abdominis muscle.

Fig. 9. Jeet Kune Do on-guard stance engaging the transverse abdominis muscle.

3   Boxing – 'Take the Tools, Throw Away the Rules'

Apart from the obvious use of boxing tools in the later development of Jeet Kune Do, little has been recorded on the underlying mechanics of boxing and its overall influence on the art of Jeet Kune Do.

Lee first studied Western boxing in the St Francis Xavier Catholic School, where he entered the school boxing programme for a short while. Brother Edward had the idea of channelling Bruce's energy into a positive form of exercise to help steer him away from street fighting. His Wing Chun teacher, Wong Shun Leung, had made a study of boxing and helped to prepare Bruce in private for a school boxing tournament. In 1958 Bruce was crowned high school boxing champion, although he resorted to his Wing Chun straight blast to overcome his final opponent.

On Lee's return to the United States he encountered many people with boxing skills; indeed, quite a few of his own students were already skilful boxers. Remembering Wong Shun Leung's earlier warning to watch out for boxers, Lee continued to research the skills of top boxers and developed ways to deal with them. What he admired about boxing was its 'aliveness', the way it flowed from movement to movement and its lack of stop/start when a point was scored, which was prevalent in the karate tournaments of the day. However, Lee felt that his own martial art training was more effective for a street fight, as it lacked the rules and regulations of the sport of boxing. Lee later took the tools of boxing but threw away the rules, which he saw as a limitation in a real fight. Foul tactics were in. Head butting, all types of holding and hitting, pulling and hitting, hitting with the elbow, forearm or open palm, hitting below the belt, the back and the back of the head, kneeing in the clinch, sweeping, wrestling and hitting while an opponent was on the ground were all frowned upon in boxing, but became legitimate techniques in Jeet Kune Do.

Further to Lee's fight with Wong Jak Man in January 1965, in which he was the victor but felt he was too out of breath afterwards, Lee investigated boxers' physical training and conditioning routines. These are explored below.

Road Work

Road work became the order of the day and Bruce would run between 1.5 miles to 3 miles a day, as well as regularly riding on an exercise bike. Included in the running were straight sprints, hill sprints and running up and down stairs, all designed to develop endurance, agility and that all-important explosiveness.

Rope Jumping – Skipping

Another great tool adopted from boxing was the use of the jump rope (see Fig. 10). Skipping became part of Lee's regular conditioning routine, being used to develop leg spring, co-ordination, strength and endurance while at the same time working arm strength.

Here are some variations in jumping rope to keep it more interesting and fun to do:

• two feet together
• one foot at a time
• knees high
• cross arms
• rope to either side
• lower body twist.

Start with three three-minute rounds, with thirty seconds' rest between each round. As this becomes too easy, increase the number of rounds or the length of each round; also try a twenty-minute skip for all-round endurance. Make the rounds challenging and try to maintain a high level of intensity.

Fig. 10. A Jeet Kune Do workout starts with skipping.

Shadow Boxing

For a boxer, shadow boxing is a means of perfecting form. Using both attacking and defensive manoeuvres, the boxer visualizes an opponent in front of himself and moves about the ring as if in a fight. Sometimes the boxer shadow-boxes in front of a full-length mirror so that he can clearly see any problems that need working on (see Figs 11–12). Once form has been corrected, speed can be increased. Lee took shadow boxing to another level, by including hand, foot, knee and elbow combinations. He would also shadow-spar while holding light handweights to increase the power and snap in his punches.

Fig. 11. Students shadow sparring in front of mirrors.

Fig. 12. Students working on various tools in front of mirrors.

Training Equipment

From the world of boxing Lee discovered the use of specific training equipment, for example the heavy bag, which was used to develop body feel and power in punching. In Bruce Lee's case, elbows, knees and kicks were developed on the bag as well (see Fig 13, overleaf).

The top and bottom ball are made of leather and attached from the ceiling by a rubber cable and from the floor by a rope or cable. The ball is positioned at chin height and various tools used to strike it. The top and bottom balls develop correct distance, timing and, above all, accuracy.

One of the most valuable training tools in Jeet Kune Do is the use of the focus pads. Lee first got the idea of the pads from British boxers and he soon adopted this versatile tool to his own training regimen. It has continued to be part of JKD training (see Figs 14–15, overleaf).

CLOCKWISE FROM TOP LEFT:

Fig. 13. Students working the heavy bags.

Fig. 14. Flashing the focus gloves.

Fig. 15. Pad man hits back to gain defensive reaction from trainee.

Footwork

A boxer's footwork allows him to move in all directions while in the ring. Lee added the circling, curving and angling footwork of boxing to his linear footwork, which he developed from fencing (see Chapter 4). Following are some footwork exercises that can be included in a JKD training regimen.

The Side Step As an opponent lunges in, step to the left with your left foot, then pivot to the right, transferring weight to the right foot so that you turn in to face your opponent on his side, then fire a cross (see Figs 16–18).

Fig. 16. On-guard right lead versus left lead.

Fig. 17. Side step against the rear straight.

Fig. 18. Pivot to the right and fire a cross.

Another method of using the side step is to slide the lead foot back first, then step out to the side with the left foot, then pivot to the right, transferring weight to the right foot. This can be done to make the opponent feel you are retreating back in a straight line, but then shifting out to the side and attacking from this new angle (see Figs 19–22).

Fig. 19. Right lead versus right lead.

Fig. 20. Opponent lunges forward. Slide your lead foot back ...

Fig. 21. … and step left foot out to the side, evading the jab.

Fig. 22. Pivot and fire the cross.

The Quarter Turn   If both fighters are in right lead on-guard stance and the opponent steps in to strike, glide the rear left foot out in an arc to face the opponent at a 90-degree angle. This movement is similar to a matador evading a charging bull (see Figs 23–25).

CLOCKWISE FROM TOP LEFT:

Fig. 23. Facing off with an opponent.

Fig. 24. Quarter turn to evade an opponent's rush …

Fig. 25. … and follow with a lead punch.

The Drop Shift When both opponents face each other in right leads and the opponent steps in to attack with a lead jab, counter by sliding the lead right foot back towards the left foot, then push off the ball of the right foot while stepping forward with the left foot switching leads, counter-punching at the same time (see Figs 26–29 and 30–32).

Fig. 26. Facing an opponent in a right on-guard stance.

Fig. 27. Opponent advances. Slide your lead foot back …

Fig. 28. … then spring forward with a drop shift …

Fig. 29. … and rear straight to the body.

Fig. 30. Right lead versus left lead.

Fig. 31. Opponent fires a rear leg round kick. Slide back the lead leg …

Fig. 32. … and drop shift, coming up on an opponent's blind side.

Angling Off

Bruce Lee discovered that the angling-off theory of boxing was the same as Wing Chun Gung Fu's theory of facing. Stepping out on a 45-degree angle to either side assists in evading a punch and also leaves an opponent out of position to hit again without turning, which allows hitting again on the half beat (see Figs 33–36).

Fig. 33. Right on guard.

Fig. 34. Opponent feeds a right punch. Angle off to the left and feed a rear straight to the body.

Fig. 35. Right on guard.

Fig. 36. Opponent feeds a rear straight. Angle off to the right and feed a right rear straight to the body.

A variation of the angle-off step is sometimes known as 'waltzing'. By stepping the rear foot out on a 45-degree angle and pivoting the lead leg back around, you will face the opponent on a 45-degree angle ready to throw a combination of blows (see Figs 37–40).

Fig. 37. Ready stance.

Fig. 38. Angle-off against the jab ...

Fig. 39. ... and rear-foot replace.

Fig. 40. Return with a rear round kick.

When facing an opponent in right lead and the opponent throws a rear straight, step the lead right foot out on a 45-degree angle, then pivot on the ball of the right foot while gliding the rear left foot out towards your right. This will bring you out facing an opponent's blind side, ready to throw a combination of blows (see Figs 41–44).

Fig. 41. On guard.

Fig. 42. Opponent feeds a rear straight. Angle off to the right ...

Fig. 43. ... and rear-foot replace.

Fig. 44. Return with a rear knee strike.

Boxers also train in ways to escape when their rear leg touches the bottom of the rope of the ring or when they get trapped in the corner on the turnbuckle. These methods of escape translate to a street confrontation when you are trapped in the corner of a room or backed up against a wall.

Combinations of the side step, quarter turn and waltz are used while covering up (see Figs 45–48).

Fig. 45. Back to the wall.

Fig. 46. Slip outside off the rear straight.

Fig. 47. Angle off to the right …

Fig. 48. … and replace the rear foot to escape.

Power

One of the skills a boxer develops is his knock-out power, which equates to: directed body mass along with strike speed equals power. The centre of mass is located in the pelvis. To learn to control this centre and to use it in all strikes is to be well on the way to developing power. Bruce Lee was a master of throwing his hips into the punch. At only 135lb he was throwing punches like a heavy-weight boxer.

Lee was greatly influenced by legendary heavyweight boxing champion Jack Dempsey, who in 1950 produced a detailed analysis of his personal boxing technique. Bruce applied Dempsey's knowledge to his own unique form, developing a devastating punch, and from Dempsey he discovered the four ways of setting his body in motion, which are set out below.

Falling forward   Raising the lead foot as you step out adds the force of gravity to the punch, relaying the whole weight of the body into the strike before the lead foot plants down on the ground (see Figs 49–50).

Springing forward   This is the same as the push-shuffle, that is, exploding forward off the ball of the rear foot (see Figs 51–52).

Fig. 49. Raise the lead foot and fall forward ...

Fig. 50. ... into the punch.

Fig. 51. Right bai-jong.

Fig. 52. Spring forward, push-shuffle.

Shoulder whirl By whirling the shoulders as you transfer weight from one foot to the other, you engage the use of the powerful back muscles (see Figs 53–54).

Surging upward Directing the body mass upward in the line of the punch creates power in the uppercut motion (see Figs 55–56).

All punches combine at least two of the above methods.

The Hinge Principle
Here, boxers imagine that the upper body is a solid door that pivots on its hinges – the hinge being the lead or rear foot. The boxer imagines that he is slamming the door shut while pivoting on the hinge of the front or rear foot (see Fig 57).

For example, the lead hook punch slams the door towards the inside of your body, twisting on the central axis line (known as the mother line in Wing Chun Gung Fu) (see Figs 58–59).

FROM TOP TO BOTTOM RIGHT:

Fig 53. On guard.
Fig. 54. Shoulder whirl with the lead hook.
Fig. 55. Dropping the right hip.
Fig. 56. Surge upward with the uppercut.

CLOCKWISE FROM TOP LEFT:

Fig. 57. Slamming the door shut to the outside.
Fig. 58. The lead hook punch.
Fig. 59. Slamming the door shut to the inside.

Acceleration

The second part of the punching equation is acceleration. To increase the speed of the punch, the arms need to remain relaxed in order to relay the force of the body mass into the punch. If the arms are stiff or tense, the antagonistic muscles are engaged and this will leave you fighting against yourself, very much like using the brakes on a car, as opposed to the analogy 'Keep your foot on the gas'. The arms should feel like the crack of a whip as you use a snap at the end of every punch, rather than a push.

Remember that directed body mass plus strike speed will develop knock-out power.

It is interesting to note that Dan Inosanto, Bruce Lee's most famous student and Sifu (teacher) at the Los Angeles China Town School, later added many boxing drills to the curriculum so that students could develop skills without always having to spar and so cutting down on injuries.

41

4　The Fencing Connection

Bruce Lee was first introduced to Western fencing by his brother Peter, a British Commonwealth Champion fencer. There has been reference made to Bruce playing slap-fighting with Peter. Slap fighting is sword fencing without the sword, using the hand instead to touch or slap one's opponent. Bruce is reported to have 'lost his cool' after being touched several times by Peter, retaliating with a straight-blast flurry of punches.

Perhaps it was Peter's skill with the blade that later led Bruce to research the tactics and strategies of fencing, especially as it was a system of fighting that had stood the test of time, with sword fencing matches being recorded as far back as 1190BC in Ancient Egypt. Amongst the books in Lee's personal library there were many volumes on Western fencing, with notes and underlinings made by him in works by great fencing masters such as Roger Crosnier, C.L. de Beaumont and Aldo Nadi. It was Bruce Lee's genius that allowed him to adapt a bladed art to that of empty hand fighting.

When Bruce looked outside of the Wing Chun system of Gung Fu, he focused on distance. Instead of playing the game of waiting for the opponent to come into the trap, he looked for a method of taking the fight to the opponent. In order to explode forward, he needed to examine his existing Wing Chun stance. Distributing most of the weight onto the rear foot, tucking the tail bone in and tilting the hips forward allowed the Wing Chun exponent to kick with ease with the lead leg, but limited his advanced forward movement. Lee's main concern was his ability to advance and retreat with great speed and to control the distance with more long-range tools. What first sprang to mind was his brother's fencing ability, the way he could close effectively from a distance and score. Bruce began to experiment with his stance, changing the weight distribution of the feet so that it was more forward and carrying his rear hand higher to protect his face.

Perhaps Lee's biggest discovery was the raised rear heel. His main influence was the fencing maestro Aldo Nadi. Contrary to other fencing masters, Nadi insisted that his students should fence with a raised rear heel, thereby taking full advantage of the spring-like mechanics of the arch of the foot. Applying pressure on the ground through the ball of the rear foot allowed Nadi to load up energy and spring forward with tremendous force.

A lot of the attributes applied to the Jeet Kune Do on-guard stance, bi-jong, were assimilated from the works of Aldo Nadi. Nadi referred to a good fencer in his on-guard position as a cobra coiled in a relaxed position, with the potential to lunge forward with the power of a released coiled spring. He believed that, like the cobra, a fencer's strike should be felt before it is seen. The left rear leg of the on-guard stance provided a lot of the power and speed for a fast attack. Nadi felt that the rear leg was the spark plug or piston of the whole fencing machine and

Diagram 4. The evolution of the Jeet Kune Do on-guard stance.

the raised rear heel was the key to his devastating explosive power.

Bruce Lee adopted the fencer's lead. Standing strong side forward, he placed his lead forearm on the runway (an imaginary line running from the lead hip to the opponent's chin), keeping his elbow approximately a fist distance away from his lead hip (see Diagram 4). The lead forearm replaced the fencer's blade. As the lead hand was closer to the opponent, it meant that this hand was predominantly used in attack and became a front-line barrier for an opponent's attempt to get past. However, it was not held so far forward as to overextend the arm, thus eliminating possible immobilization attacks on the limb.

Distance

This new on-guard stance allowed Lee to advance and strike from non-attachment and be outside of his opponent's reach. For this strategy to be effective one needs to be able to control distance.

In Western fencing the distance maintained between two fencers during a bout is known as the 'fencing measure'. In Jeet Kune Do this became known as the 'fighting measure'. The fencing/fighting measure can be broken down into three measures, the first being called 'out of distance'. At this range, an opponent can be touched by first taking a step and then lunging forward. The second measure is known as 'correct distance'. Here the opponent can be touched with a simple lunge. Finally, the third measure is known as 'close distance', as the opponent can now be reached without lunging.

It soon became apparent that the determining factor of superiority is to be aware of distance at all times – the person controlling this distance controls the fight. Having a keen sense of the different fighting measures and correct judgment of distance while facing an opponent in relation to one's own tools, and the speed with which they can be delivered, became a deciding factor regarding the optimal fighting measure.

Footwork

In fencing, both opponents try to outmanoeuvre each other in order to be at the right distance to score. This is achieved by a unique form of linear footwork known as 'gaining and breaking ground'. Most of the linear footwork in Jeet Kune Do was adapted from Western fencing. While maintaining good balance, the fighters vary the length and speed of their steps in order to deceive one another's range, bringing them off balance and scoring at their moment of vulnerability.

Short, light steps are used to maintain the desired range from an opponent, keeping oneself out of an opponent's range, but not too far so that one is unable to close the gap with a quick lunge attack. In Jeet Kune Do, these short steps are known as the 'shuffle', or 'step and slide' (see *Jeet Kune Do – A Core Structure Training Manual*).

In fencing, the lunge forms the basis of all attack, the sword arm moving first followed by the lead leg striding out. In Jeet Kune Do, the lunge is known as the 'push-shuffle' advance, which is an explosive lunge forward of the ball of the foot of the rear leg. The lead hand moving ahead of the lead foot forms the foundation of the attack (see Figs 60–61).

Fig. 60. On guard.

Fig. 61. Lead straight lunge.

When fighting against a fencer that keeps a good fencing measure, always retreating on one's advance and seeming to be always out of distance, a running attack called a 'fleche' can be used. The 'fleche' is achieved by leaning forward and bringing oneself off balance, thus adding to the forward momentum. As the weight of the body comes onto the lead leg, the rear foot steps through in a running motion, covering a greater distance and catching an opponent off guard. In empty hand combat the fleche motion is used in a similar fashion, only without the continued running motion. Against an opponent who always shifts back against your lead leg stepping forward, the fleche can be used to deceive the range. By leaning the upper torso forward and extending the lead hand, slightly pulling yourself off balance, the rear foot steps up level with your calf, then the ball of the foot touches down just in front of your lead foot, creating a spring from which to push forward as the lead foot strides out and covers a greater distance (see Figs 62–65).

Fig. 62. On guard.

Fig. 63. Leaning forward to add to forward momentum.

Fig. 64. Rear leg comes up level with your calf, then touches down, creating a springboard to push forward ...

Fig. 65. ... into a lead-hand strike.

The idea of deceiving an opponent by varying the distance of the steps became an integral part of Jeet Kune Do's identity. As Bruce Lee said, 'The essence of fighting is the art of moving.' If an opponent is difficult to reach on one's advance because of his fine sense of controlling the distance, it becomes possible to draw the opponent forward by varying the distance of the rear foot while stepping back (breaking ground) until the opponent is lulled into the range of the lunge and scored on (see Figs 66–69).

Fig. 66. On guard.
Fig. 67. Step and slide back, opponent steps and slides forward.

Fig. 68. A short rear step back draws an opponent forward ...

Fig. 69. ... into a lead straight.

On the other hand, if one has an opponent that always retreats out of distance whenever an attempt to attack is made, it is possible to deceive him by stealing a step, once again varying the distance of the feet. This time, the rear foot is brought closer to the lead foot on the recovery of an attacking tool, bringing the attacker closer to the opponent as his second attack scores on the lead leg step out. In fencing terms, this tactic is known as 'gaining on the lunge'. In Jeet Kune Do it is called a simple 'slide step' (see Figs 70–73).

Fig. 70. On guard.

Fig. 71. Step and slide forward, opponent retreats.

Fig 72. On the next step and slide forward, the rear leg is brought closer ...

Fig. 73. ... bringing you closer for the lead straight.

Varying distance of steps in a broken rhythm fashion will help to control the fighting measure by adding the element of deception, catching an opponent off guard and forcing him to make errors of judgment. A good drill is to imagine that the floor is red hot and you cannot stand in one place for too long for fear of burning the soles of your feet. This will instil the idea of small, constant, purposeful movement.

Targets

When a fencer takes his on-guard stance with his blade facing towards an opponent, the areas above his sword are known as the 'high lines' and the areas below as the 'low lines'. These target areas are then divided down the middle by an imaginary line, creating four distinct areas called quarte, sixte, septime and octave. The target areas on the outside of the sword arm are called 'outside lines' and the target areas inside of the sword arm are 'inside lines'. When further divided, this gives the fencer high inside, high outside, low inside and low outside areas to defend. Lee was already familiar with this framework structure of defence from his Wing Chun training. It was known as the four gates and later in Jeet Kune Do as the four corners (see Diagram 5).

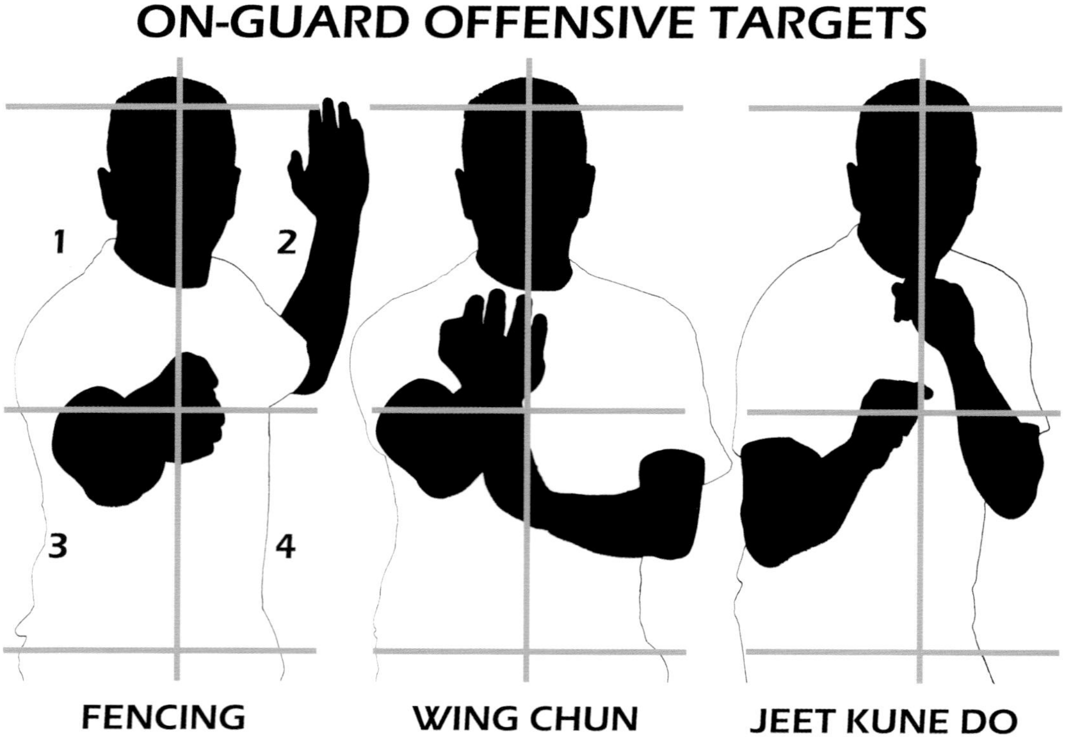

ON-GUARD OFFENSIVE TARGETS

FENCING **WING CHUN** **JEET KUNE DO**

Diagram 5. The areas of defence.

Defence

The fencer defends the four areas by use of a parry with his blade against an incoming attack. By taking his on-guard position he automatically covers one line with his sword arm. The remaining lines are covered with a variety of parries, simple parries, semicircular parries or circular parries. In Jeet Kune Do both hands are free to parry, although the rear hand has a more prominent role as a defensive tool that is able to be used as an attacking weapon as well, much like the espada y daga, or 'sword and dirk', old school of Spanish fencing. Here, the fencer held a dagger in the rear hand and used it to deflect incoming attacks as well as to thrust at targets of opportunity.

Simple parries use the sword hand to deflect incoming thrusts by moving laterally across the body (see Figs 74–75).

Fig. 74. On guard.

Fig. 75. A simple cross parry.

Semicircular parries scribe a semicircular motion from a high to a low line, or a low line to a high line (see Figs 76–78).

Fig. 76. On guard facing an opponent.

Fig 77. High ...

Fig. 78. ... to low semicircular parries.

Circular parries form a complete circle, bringing the blade back to the original point of engagement. For empty hand purposes circular parries become more apparent in clinch situations, in which both opponents have clashed arms together and are seeking to open a line of attack (see Figs 79–81).

Fig. 79 Engagement on the outside.

Fig. 80. Opponent disengages and circles outside, counter circle ...

Fig. 81. ... ending in the original line of engagement.

Attack

Bruce Lee divided attacking strategies into groups known as 'the five ways of attack': single direct /single angular attack; attack by combination; hand immobilization attack; progressive indirect attack; and attack by drawing, all of which he came across in his fencing studies.

Single Direct Attack/Single Angular Attack

The single direct attack in Jeet Kune Do came from the idea of fencing's simple attack, which was a single blade movement made at targets of opportunity. Simple attacks can be direct or indirect. A direct attack in fencing is a straight thrust to the target with no attempt to disguise the line of attack. An indirect attack is a single blade movement that travels over or under an opponent's blade to score in an open line.

In Jeet Kune Do, a single direct attack is the same as fencing's simple attack (see Figs 82–83) and the fencer's indirect attack became known as single indirect attack (see Figs 84–85), an attack that angles the body by leaning the trunk and angulating the footwork to shift the body while hitting in a direct line.

Fig. 82. On guard facing an opponent.

Fig. 83. Single direct front instep kick to the groin.

Fig. 84. On guard.

Fig. 85. Step of angulated side kick.

Attack by Combination

Attack by combination consists of two or more strikes that are intended to land on an opponent. This type of attack can be fired at more than one target.

The closest method in fencing to this is the compound attack, which uses several offensive movements of attack. The first move is called a feint, which is a motion that is designed to gain a reaction from an opponent in order to score in another line. A compound attack is used when a fencer runs into difficulty scoring with his simple attack. The complexity of a compound attack relates to an opponent's ability to parry the fencer's simple attacks (see *Jeet Kune Do – A Core Structure Training Manual*).

Hand Immobilization Attack

Bruce Lee was already well grounded in the skills of trapping from his constant chi-sau sticking hands practice that formed a major part of his early Wing Chun Gung Fu training.

The 'engagement' of blades in fencing gave Lee a way to take his trapping skills out of chi-sau into a more combative realm. The cross blade position of fencing became the lead-hand outside 'reference point' and in Jeet Kune Do this was the starting point from which to learn the hand immobilization attack (see Fig 86).

Fig. 86. High outside reference position.

The contact of the blades enables a fencer to feel his opponent's movements and intentions – this is known as 'sentiment du fer'. When the blades are engaged the line of attack is closed and, in order to score, a change of engagement is needed by circling under or over an opponent's blade, trying to open a line of attack. This is the same route motion as the heun-san circling hand motion in Wing Chun Gung Fu (see Figs 87–89).

Fig. 87. High reference.

Fig. 88. Huen-san small disengagement ...

Fig. 89. ... to biu-jee finger jab.

Attacks on the Blade The beat, the pressure, the bind, the croisé and the envelopment are all considered attacks on the blade and involve some kind of contact reflex against the weapon.

The Beat The beat is used to knock aside an opponent's blade that will not respond to feints. It is used to open a line of attack, or gain a reaction back so that it can be disengaged and an attack made in the opening line (see Figs 90–92).

Fig. 90. The beat on an opponent's lead arm ...

Fig. 91. ... gains a reaction back ...

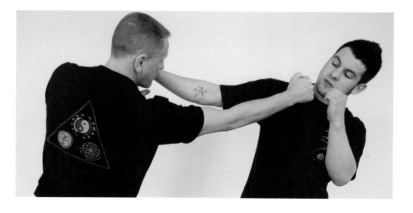

Fig. 92. ... that is disengaged and the lead straight thrown.

The Pressure When both blades are engaged in contact with each other, the pressure is used to press against the opposing blade, either to open a line, or to gain counter-pressure back so that it can be deceived with a disengagement (see Figs 93–95).

Fig. 93. A long-range clinch.

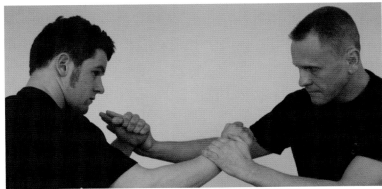

Fig. 94. Apply pressure on opponent's rear hand ...

Fig. 95. ... gaining counter-pressure that is disengaged and scored on the inside line.

The Bind The bind engages the opponent's blade and guides it diagonally from the high line to the low line, or the low line to the high line (see Figs 96–98).

Fig. 96. Inside forearms clash.

Fig. 97. Circle arm over and diagonally down.

Fig. 98. Opening a low line groin shot.

The Croisé The croisé is a circular motion over an opponent's blade with a downward force being applied taking the opponent's blade down on the same side of the target (see Figs 99–102).

Fig. 99. By crashing in on an opponent you gain an outside high engagement …

Fig. 100. … which is circled and pressed down on the same side as the body …

Fig. 101. … to an under hook control …

Fig. 102. … to a bent arm lock.

The Envelopment The envelopment forces both blades to make a circular motion while maintaining contact, bringing the attacking blade on top in the strongest position in the original line of engagement (see Figs 103–105).

Fig. 103. The engagement.

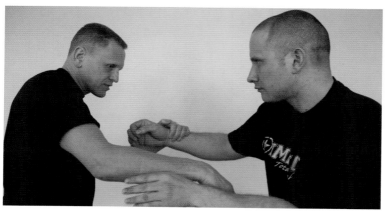

Fig. 104. Enveloping the opponent's arm.

Fig. 105. Both arms circle without losing contact, bringing the arm back in the strongest position.

Progressive Indirect Attack

Against an opponent who is difficult to hit with simple attacks, a fencer uses a method of attack known as a 'progressive attack'. This is a form of compound attack, the first part being a feint followed by the real attack with no retraction of the weapon. The tip of the blade continues to move forward towards the target. The first part of the attack covers half of the distance towards the opponent. The feint draws the opponent's blade away from the real intended target; having gained time and keeping the attacking blade ahead of an opponent's blade, he attacks in the open line. In Jeet Kune Do, this form of attack became known as the 'progressive indirect attack', also referred to as 'second intention' (see Figs 106–108 and 109–111).

Fig. 106. On guard.

Fig. 107. Feinting the front kick gains a reaction from an opponent's rear hand.

Fig. 108 Change the line of attack with a lead hook kick.

Fig. 109. On guard.

Fig. 110. Feint a lead hand to the solar plexis as an opponent starts to parry with his lead hand.

Fig. 111. Throw a cross into the opening line.

Attack by Drawing

Fencers sometimes open a line of attack in order to draw an attack from an opponent. This is called an 'invitation' in fencing and in Jeet Kune Do 'attack by drawing'. Here a target is exposed to gain a predictable response from an opponent (see Figs 112–114).

Fig. 112. Right lead versus left lead.

Fig. 113. Raise the rear elbow to draw the opponent's rear-hand strike.

Fig. 114. As he takes the bait, throw the rear cross.

Second Intention

Second intention is also known as a 'renewed attack', a second offensive movement made immediately after the first attack fails to reach the target, or is parried on the way. In fencing, there are three ways to renew the attack: the remise; the redoublement; and the reprise.

The Remise   The remise is the renewal of the thrust in the same line of attack with no withdrawal of the blade and is used against a fencer who parries the first attack, but fails to counter-attack immediately (see Figs 115–118).

Fig. 115. On guard.

Fig. 116. Feed a lead jab; opponent covers.

Fig. 117. Immediately shove the lead hand back into his face.

Fig. 118. Setting up a rear cross.

The Redoublement The redoublement is a renewal of attack that changes the line of attack on the second movement while continuing the forward motion of the lunge (see Figs 119–121).

Fig. 119. On guard facing an opponent.

Fig. 120. The lead jab is parried.

Fig. 121. Immediately change lines and strike the body.

The Reprise This is a renewal of attack made after returning to the on-guard position. If the opponent retreats or parries an attack, then retreats, the fencer comes back on-guard momentarily then relaunches his attack (see Figs 122–125).

Fig. 122. On guard.

Fig. 123. Opponent parries the lead lunge.

Fig. 124. Momentarily come back to on guard position ...

Fig. 125. ... and relaunch the lead jab.

Counter-Attack

Counter-attack takes the form of defensive/offensive action, or an offensive action against an opponent's attack.

The Riposte   In fencing, the parry deflects the attack, which is followed very quickly by the defender turning his parry into an attack known as a 'riposte'. The riposte can be direct or indirect; direct in the same line as the parry, or indirect disengaging into another line of attack. The counter can be returned from a stationary position called pied ferme, or with the advancing footwork depending on the distance and reaction of the opponent (see Figs 126–127 and 128–130).

Fig. 128. Unmatched leads.

Fig. 126. Inside parry.

Fig. 129. The opponent's lead jab to the body is covered with a lead-hand jum-sau.

Fig. 127. Riposte with a back fist.

Fig. 130. To a lead straight.

Fig. 131. Opponent gives away his intention to attack.

Fig. 132. He is intercepted with a side kick.

Fig. 133. On guard.

Fig. 134. Rear bridge punch.

The Stop-Hit The stop-hit is designed to strike the opponent before his attack arrives, therefore it is an attack on his preparation. As an opponent steps forward he gets hit, or as he begins to strike you intercept with a strike of your own arriving first (see Figs 131–132). Lee came to regard the stop-hit/kick as the highest form of defence, being the most direct way to counter-fight an opponent.

Time-Hit The time-hit is a parry–reposte movement made at the same time, deflecting the attacker's blade. As the defender slides his blade forward along his opponent's blade, he creates a deflective force that impales his opponent on the tip of his blade (see Figs 133–134).

Counter Time Counter time is used against an opponent who has formed a habit of stop-hitting your every move. It is a form of second intention, used to draw out an opponent's stop-hit so that the fencer can parry it and riposte (see Figs 135–138). The stop-hit can be drawn in various ways that include moving forward while uncovered, inviting an

Fig. 135. On guard facing an opponent.

Fig. 136. Every time you move in, your opponent attempts to stop-hit.

Fig. 137. On your second attempt to move in ...

Fig. 138. ... you draw an opponent's stop-hit and evade with a counter time-hit of your own.

attack by opening a line and feinting an attack with a bent arm. If the attempt to draw the stop-hit is not convincing enough, an opponent may not give you the reaction you want, or he may use his stop-hit as a feint to draw your parry. This is how the fight takes the form of a game of chess, as two skilled opponents try to outmanoeuvre each other.

Rhythm, Cadence and Tempo

Bruce Lee gained many principles and tactics from fencing that proved to be universal, regardless of whether fighting with a sword or empty-handed. Rhythmic and non-rhythmic movement, the changing of cadence and the ideal moment to strike, known as 'tempo', are all drawn from Western fencing.

To understand timing in fencing, all movements are broken down into beats, or units of movement time. A group of recurring beats at the same pace is known to be in rhythm. In Jeet Kune Do, the idea of rhythm is recognized in fighters who throw a steady diet of tools at the same pace, for example a combination of jab–cross–hook is a rhythm of one–two–three. The Jeet Kune Do exponent tries to read his opponent's rhythm, while at the same time being aware of his own. A keen awareness of rhythm leads to the ability of being able to break rhythm.

The speed of the rhythm is known as the 'cadence'. Adjusting one's own cadence to fit in with an opponent's is the skill of the fencer. Once you have imposed your cadence on an opponent it is possible to change pace by speeding up, leaving an opponent moving too slowly to defend. This is known as a 'touch on time'; that one beat in a cadence that catches an opponent at his point of vulnerability is known as 'tempo'. Another way to break rhythm is to feed a combination with a fast cadence, then

Fig. 139. On guard.

Fig. 140. Parry an opponent's jab.

suddenly slow down or pause a movement. This is called 'broken time' in fencing and it disrupts an opponent's timing so that he momentarily leaves a line open that can be scored in.

Half Beats

It is possible to break an opponent's rhythm by hitting on the half beat. Remember a rhythm of 'one and two and three'. It is a three beat rhythm with the strike landing on the 'and' between the beats. This catches an opponent between the two movements (see Figs 139–141).

It is impossible not to realize the connection and importance that Bruce Lee gave to the tactics and strategies of blade fighting. In one's own research, it is helpful to be aware that most fencing is done with the single lead hand, but in empty hand fighting these same principles can apply to both the lead and rear hands and legs.

Fig. 141. Intercept on the half beat with a lead straight as the opponent starts to rear hook.

5   Hand Tools

The hand tools not discussed in this book are the lead straight, the straight Blast, jik-chung-chuie, the finger jab biu-jee, JKD long hook and the JKD long shovel. All of the above have been comprehensively covered in *Jeet Kune Do – A Core Structure Manual*. Following are the remaining hand tools to add to the Jeet Kune Do arsenal of attack.

Lead Jab

This is the bread and butter tool of Western boxing and the most frequently used in a boxing match. From the on-guard stance, snap out the lead hand in a straight line with a quarter turn of the lead shoulder. As the arm reaches about 95 per cent of the way out, rotate the palm downward, facing the floor. The chin should be tucked inside the lead shoulder and the rear hand kept up, protecting the side of the face. After contact is made, the arm should retract along the same line, taking care not to drop the hand down on the way back (see Figs 142–143).

There are various types of jab. The first is the flicker jab, which lacks power. Thrown out from the elbow at a fast speed, it is used as a

Fig. 142. On guard.

Fig. 143. Lead jab.

feeler to see how an opponent reacts, or as a range finder to set up other tools. Sometimes it is used to disguise an advancing forward step to close the gap for a kick (see Figs 144–146).

Fig. 144. On guard at long range.

Fig. 145. Flicker jab used to disguise lead step ...

Fig. 146. ... to set up a lead hook kick to the groin.

The second type of jab is the speed jab. This generates power by throwing the shoulder forward while adding a short step forward. It is used to keep an opponent off balance, or stop him from coming forward.

The third method is the power jab. Driven from the pivot of the rear foot, it transfers energy from the ground up through the hip and shoulder and out through the fist. The power punch can also be applied by taking a step forward, pushing off the rear ball of the foot.

Jab to the Body

Stepping forward with the lead foot, bend the lead leg slightly and the rear leg even more, then bring the body down so that the shoulder lines up with the punch. Tilt the head slightly to the side, keeping the rear hand in front of the face. Power is obtained by leaning the body forward and turning the shoulder into the punch. This punch can be used to bring an opponent's guard down, opening up the high line (see Fig 147).

Fig. 147. Jab to the body.

Lead Hook

The lead hook adds a curved angle to an attack. It is mainly used as a counter-punch, or as a follow-up to the jab or cross. The lead arm is bent, so can be thrown outside of an opponent's vision, catching him on the side of the head. Power comes from the rotation of the lead side of the body as the weight transfers from the front to the rear foot. The lead foot pivots on the ball, the hip and lead shoulder turn inward, bringing the lead arm around parallel to the floor. Keeping the lead-hand knuckles facing the same direction as the body's twisting motion drives the fist through the centre line (see Fig 148).

Fig. 148. Lead hook.

The lead hook can be thrown at close, medium or long range (see Figs 149–151).The close-range hook is used for infighting and can be thrown while in the clinch. The medium-range hook is probably the most powerful, as you are at a distance to get full use of the transfer of weight and full pivot of the body, resulting in a potential knock-out punch. The long-range hook can catch out an opponent as he expects straight shots at the long range.

CLOCKWISE FROM TOP LEFT:

Fig. 149. Close-range hook.

Fig. 150. Medium-range hook.

Fig. 151. Long-range hook.

Lead Body Hook

The lead body hook is used for inside fighting. It usually follows some kind of evasion of an opponent's tools to bring you close in. Using the same mechanics as the high lead hook, the body pivots inward. The difference between the high and low hook is the positioning of the elbow. In body hooking the elbow is kept in closer to the body, so that the lead arm and body pivot turn as one unit (see Fig 152).

Fig. 152. Lead body hook.

A good exercise for the body hook is to hold a focus pad under the armpit as you practise the pivot motion to strike an opponent or focus pad, the goal being not to drop the pad that is under the arm. This exercise develops good mechanics (see Figs 153–154).

Fig. 153. Start with a focus pad under your right armpit.

Fig. 154. Perform a body hook without dropping the pad.

Lead Uppercut

The lead uppercut is a good close-in tool for infighting. It travels upward in a straight line, striking under the chin or solar plexis. Keeping both arms tucked in, bend the knees and lean slightly to the side you are going to punch with. Transfer your weight to the back foot and raise the lead hip upward, exploding towards the target and driving the arm up the opponent's centre line. The fist makes contact with the palm side of the hand facing back to you. Care must be taken to keep the wrist in line with the forearm so that it is not damaged. Dropping the forearm down in order to swing it upward will expose too much of your own targets (see Fig 155).

Qua Chuie Backfist

The backfist is thrown on the same line as the lead straight. Turning the hip sharply in the opposite direction at the last moment changes the angle of the attack and causes

Fig. 155. Lead uppercut.

the hit to land on the side of the face. Target areas are the temple, cheek bone, nose or ear. The power comes from the hip twist and snapping extension of the elbow as the weight comes on to the front foot. Strike with the knuckles and not the back of the hand. The backfist can also be thrown from the low hand position along the left runway (see Figs 156–157) and can be used as a good follow-up from a low side kick to bring the body back in line.

Lead Corkscrew Punch

The lead corkscrew punch opens up the inside line sliding along the inside of an opponent's rear hand if both fighters are in matched leads. The lead arm travels forward as the elbow is flicked up and the body is dropped by bending the knees. The palm rotates outwards to the side. This punch is sometimes called a bent arm jab (see Fig 158).

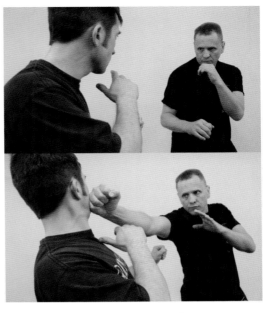

Fig. 156. Right hand held on left runway.
Fig. 157. Lead backfist.

Lead Hammer Fist

The lead hammer fist is used against an opponent who is always slipping and bobbing his way in. The contact area is the bottom of the fist, which is used in a hammering downward fashion. The hammer can be thrown as either a forehand (see Figs 159–160), or backhand strike (see Figs 161–162, overleaf).

Fig. 158. Lead corkscrew punch.

Fig. 159. Set up for lead forehand hammer fist.

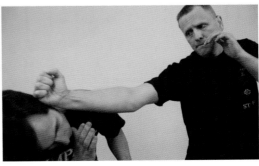

Fig. 160. Lead hammer fist.

Fig. 161. Opponent slips to the outside.

Fig. 162. Fire a backhand hammer fist.

Fig. 163. Lead hooking palm strike.

Fig. 164. Rear straight.

Lead Hooking Palm

The lead hooking palm strike is thrown from a low hand position in an arcing motion similar to the lead hook punch. The striking area is the heel of the palm and the mechanics of the body are the same as the lead hook punch (see Fig 163).

Rear Straight

The rear straight is thrown out in a straight line. Transferring weight over to the front foot, the hips twist and the shoulder turns, driving the fist forward as the rear ball of the foot digs into the ground. The lead hand pulls back to protect the side of the face and the lead elbow is tucked into the body. The other side of the jaw is protected by the rear shoulder and is like looking down the sights of the barrel of a rifle (see Fig 164).

Rear Straight to the Body

The mechanics of the rear straight to the body are the same as the rear straight on the high line. Bend the knees so that the shoulder is in line with the target and feed the arm out in a straight line (see Fig 165).

Rear Cross

The rear cross is similar to the rear straight used while slipping to the inside of an opponent's punch. The cross travels over the opponent's arm, striking from the outside. Sometimes the arm is slightly curved, allowing it to clear over the opponent's punch (see Fig 166).

Fig. 165. Rear straight to the body.

Rear Hook

The rear hook, like the lead hook, is a punch thrown outside of the line of vision that is used to go around an opponent's guard. The rear hip and shoulder rotate inward while bringing the punching arm around in a curved motion. At the same time, dig in the rear ball of the foot into the ground (see Fig 167).

Fig. 166. Rear cross.

Rear Body Hook

The rear body hook, like the lead body hook, pivots the hips and shoulder inward into the strike and can be used while slipping an opponent's punch, or as a strike as you come out of a bob and weave (see Fig 168).

Rear Uppercut

The rear uppercut is delivered by dropping the rear shoulder down, then launching the rear hip upward and driving the rear fist upward in a straight line towards the target with an explosive thrust from the rear leg and rear ball of the foot. Make sure that the forearm is not dropped down, thereby avoiding the exposing of any targets (see Fig 169).

CLOCKWISE FROM TOP LEFT:

Fig. 167. Rear hook.
Fig. 168. Rear hook to the body.
Fig. 169. Rear uppercut.

Fig. 170. Rear corkscrew punch.

Fig. 171. Rear overhead.

Rear Corkscrew Punch

The rear corkscrew punch is the same as the lead. Bend the knees and flick the rear elbow up as the fist rotates over and drives forward. Keep the head tucked inside the shoulder (see Fig 170).

Rear Overhead

The rear overhead is a curving motion blow that travels upward then downward towards the target. Like the rear cross, it can be used to pass over an opponent's punch or guard and can be used to catch an opponent as he attempts to bob and weave a lead hook (see Fig 171).

Rear Hammer Fist

The rear hammer fist uses the bottom of the hand in a hammering fashion. Like the lead hammer, it is used against an opponent who crouches down on advance, or uses a lot of slipping and bobbing on the way in (see Figs 172– 173 and 174 –175).

Fig. 172. Lead-hand parry ...

Fig. 173. ... to rear backhand hammer fist.

Fig. 174. Lead-hand parry ...

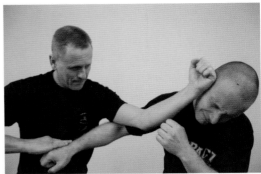

Fig. 175. ... to rear forehand hammer fist.

Rear-Hand Backfist

The rear-hand backfist is sometimes used when the left side of the body is twisting forward. Bring the rear shoulder inward towards the centre line with the rear hand slightly in front, then the backfist is thrown from an angle towards the opponent. It can be used to set up a lead hook, or for hand immobilization to clear an opponent's guard (see Figs 176–177 and 178–180).

Fig. 176. Cross-arm guard.

Fig. 177. Rear-hand backfist.

Fig. 178. Cross-arm guard.

Fig. 179. Rear-hand backfist runs into opponent's rear arm cover.

Fig. 180. Counter lop-sau chung-chuie.

Spinning Backfist

The spinning backfist can be done with the lead or the rear hand and is set up by first throwing a lead shot or after parrying an opponent's punch. The spinning backfist is a powerful blow that can catch an opponent off guard. Care must be taken when launching this attack as it can expose your back to an opponent. If too close, the forearm can be used as the striking weapon (see Figs 181–183 and 184–186).

Fig. 181. Opponent's jab is parried on the inside.

Fig. 182. Using the momentum of the parry, spin your body around ...

Fig. 183. ... and fire a rear spinning backfist.

Fig. 184. Sensing an opponent behind, glance over your shoulder …

Fig. 185. … spinning your body backward.

Fig. 186. Fire a lead-hand spinning backfist.

Rear Hooking Palm

The rear hooking palm is a curved strike with the rear hand. It is thrown like the rear overhead, striking with the heel of the palm (see Fig 187).

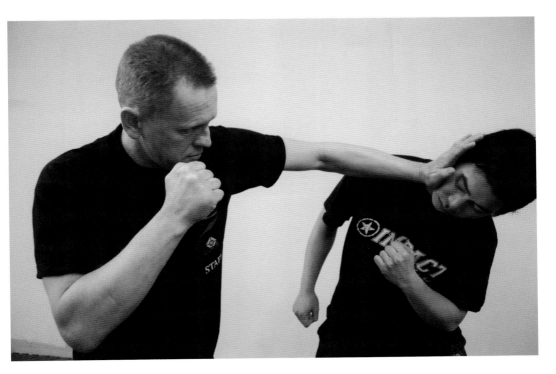

Fig. 187. Rear hooking palm.

6   Close-In Tools

Knees, Elbows, Head and Forearms

Knees

The knee strike can strike upward, downward, sideward and forward. The knee is a naturally strong weapon and can be a devastating strike.

The upward knee travels in a straight line upward, first pulling an opponent's head downward and then driving the knee up to its target (see Fig 188).

The forward or straight knee drives forward into the stomach, groin or thigh of an opponent and can be thrown from attachment or non-attachment (see Fig 189).

The sideward or curved knee is thrown from the clinch position (see Figs 190–191).

The downward knee is used against an opponent who has been taken down to the ground. It is often a good follow-up from a throw (see Figs 192–193).

Fig. 188. Upward knee.

Fig. 189. Forward knee.

Fig. 190. Set-up for curve knee.

Fig. 191. Curved knee.

Fig. 192. Opponent is thrown to the floor.

Fig. 193. Downward knee.

Elbows

The elbow can be thrown with either the lead or the rear arm in a downward, upward, sideward, rear high, rear low or spinning back fashion.

The downward elbow is often thrown from the rear arm travelling in a 45-degree angle to the target. The tip of the elbow is the striking area, with the target areas being the temple, eyebrows, cheekbone and nose (see Fig 194).

The elbow can also be thrown in a straight-down motion, driving the elbow into the head and body of a downed opponent while holding him in side control (see Figs 195–196).

It can be driven directly into the spine of an opponent who is shooting in to take you down (see Figs 197–198).

The sideward elbow is a move from the side of the body, using the same mechanics as the lead hook. Snapping the open hand in towards your chest with a short arc increases the power of the strike at close range (see Fig 199).

Fig. 194. Downward elbow strike.

Fig. 195. Side control on the ground.

Fig. 196. Downward elbow.

Fig. 197. Opponent attempts to shoot in.

Fig. 198. Sprawl back and drop a downward elbow.

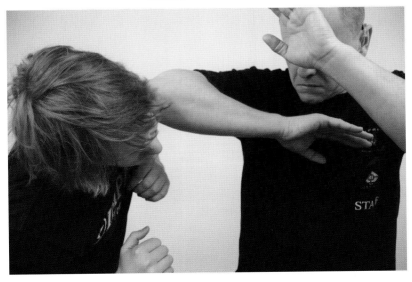

Fig. 199. Sideward elbow.

The upward elbow can travel vertically or diagonally upward towards the target following the same line as the uppercut and catching the opponent under the chin (see Fig 200).

The high rear elbow is thrown against an opponent attempting to grab you from the rear (see Fig 201).

The low rear elbow is thrown at waist height and sets up an escape from a rear bearhug (see Figs 202–203).

The spinning elbow is thrown the same way as the spinning backfist, only at a closer range (see Figs 204–206).

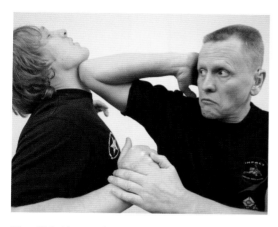

Fig. 200. Upward elbow.

Fig. 202. Opponent grabs you from behind.

Fig. 201. High-rear elbow.

CLOCKWISE FROM TOP LEFT:

Fig. 203. Drop down into a good base and rear-low elbow.

Fig. 204. Opponent throws a rear straight.

Fig. 205. Outside forearm cover as you start to spin.

Fig. 206. Spinning elbow lands.

The Elbow Flow Drill The elbow flow drill is a shadow boxing drill for solo practice. The elbow strikes in all directions and should be done on both sides (see Figs 207–211).

Fig. 207. Upward elbow.

Fig. 208. Downward elbow.

CLOCKWISE FROM TOP LEFT:

Fig. 209. Rear high elbow.

Fig. 210. High sideward elbow.

Fig. 211. Rear low elbow.

Head

The head butt can be used in a forward, upward, sideward and backwards motion (see Figs 212–215).

Fig. 212. Forward.

Fig. 213. Upward.

Fig. 214. Sidewards.

Fig. 215. Backward.

Forearms

The forearm smash is used either in a fore-hand or backhand motion. Also, when using a spinning backfist or spinning elbow, the forearm can catch the opponent as he moves in against the backfist or out against the elbow strike. The forearm can also be used from the clinch position to open a line of attack (see Figs 216–218).

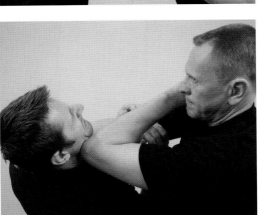

CLOCKWISE FROM TOP LEFT:

Fig. 216. From fifty/fifty clinch position.

Fig. 217. Lead forearm smash ...

Fig. 218. ... to set up elbow strike.

7   Advanced Kicking

Some of the major kicking techniques were covered in *Jeet Kune Do – A Core Structure Training Manual*. The remaining kicks are considered more advanced and rely on good balance and flexibility. They offer an opponent more opportunity to counter – for example, bringing the leg above the waist can give the opponent a chance to capture the leg and take you down. There is also the danger of having your back to an opponent when attacking with any of the turning, spinning kicks. On the plus side, these kicks can generate tremendous force.

Lead Hooking Kick

If you are in a right lead bai-jong stance, the lead hooking heel kick starts out along the line of the lead hook kick. The leg then circles outwards to the left side and whips back in across the face, striking with the heel of the foot (see Figs 219–221). The lead hooking heel kick can be dropped in a downward hooking motion to the inside of the knee, breaking an opponent's base.

Fig. 219. On guard.

Fig. 220. Lead leg travels forward...

Fig. 221. ...to lead hooking kick.

Spinning Back Kick

From the right lead on-guard stance, spin inward on the balls of the feet until you are facing to the rear. Look over your left shoulder and kick back with the left leg in a side-kick fashion, thrusting the leg straight out (see Figs 222–224).

Fig. 222. On guard facing an opponent.

Fig. 223. Spinning back to look over shoulder.

Fig. 224. Fire a rear back kick.

Fig. 238. Post on your right hand and right kick to opponent's knee.

Fig. 239. Slide right foot back, forming a tripod base.

Fig. 240. Back to standing position.

Fig. 241. Opponent attacks you while you are on the ground.

Fig. 242. Form a shell defence to a tripod base.

Fig. 243. Back to standing position.

On the other side of the coin is the ability to take an opponent down with a double leg tackle, single leg tackle or a throw (see Figs 244–247 and 248–253).

Fig. 244. Correct distance measured with the lead hand.

Fig. 245. Lower base ...

Fig. 246. ... and shoot in.

Fig. 247. Takedown, trapping the single leg.

Fig. 248. Taking the correct measure.

Fig. 249. Lower base …

Fig. 250. … and shoot in, controlling both of the opponent's legs.

Fig. 251. Bump the opponent to the side as you step up.

Fig. 252. Lift and turn.

Fig. 253. Drop the opponent, trapping both of his legs.

Grappling Attacks

Jeet Kune Do also includes all kinds of joint manipulation, locks and levers and attacks against the face, neck, shoulder, elbow, wrist, trunk, knee, ankle and toe while standing or on the ground.

Attacking the Face and Neck Attacks to the neck can be done standing or on the ground, and can be done in the form of a choke, strangle or crank (see Figs 254–260).

Fig. 254. From fifty/fifty clinch position, pop up the opponent's arm ...

Fig. 255. ... and go side naked choke.

Fig. 256. Rear naked choke.

113

Fig. 257. Front choke.

Fig. 258. Rear naked choke from the back on the ground with hooks in.

Fig. 259. Choke while the opponent is in turtle position.

Fig. 260. The opponent is inside your guard front guillotine choke.

If an opponent tucks his head in to protect his neck or throat, it is possible to use the thumb side of the wrist to face-lock an opponent (see Fig 261).

Attacks on the Shoulder and Elbow
Some attacks will immobilize the shoulder joint, while attacking the elbow and twisting the arm will also inflict pain to the shoulder. Sometimes a lever is applied to hyper-extend the elbow joint. Shoulder and elbow attacks can be done standing or from the ground (see Figs 262–268).

Fig. 261. Face lock.

Fig. 262. Shoulder, elbow and wrist lock.

Fig. 263. Reverse straight arm bar plus wrist lock.

CLOCKWISE FROM TOP LEFT:

Fig. 264. Figure four arm lock with elbow strike.

Fig. 265. Mounted arm bar.

Fig. 266. Arm bar.

Fig. 267. Omoplata arm lock.

Fig. 268. Kimura arm lock.

Attacking the Trunk The trunk is controlled by a body lock. While standing, the body lock is applied by feeding your arm around an opponent's waist and clasping your wrist. Squeezing upward and inward will break an opponent's balance and set up a takedown (see Fig 269). The body lock can also be applied while on the ground by using the legs (see Fig 270).

Fig. 269. Standing body lock.

Fig. 270. Body lock from the rear on the ground with collar and arm choke.

Attacking the Leg Attacks to the leg can be broken down into various elements. Knee bars will hyper-extend the knee joint (see Figs 271–280) and attacks to the ankle can immobilize the joint, plus with an added twist this can also affect the knee (see Fig 276).

The foot can be trapped under your armpit while you stretch the Achilles tendon (see Fig 275).

The foot can be attacked by clasping the toes with the hand and snaking the ankle with the other arm to apply a toe and ankle lock (see Fig 278).

Fig. 271. On guard facing an opponent.

Fig. 272. Catch the opponent's rear round kick while stepping to the side.

Fig. 273. Control the opponent's neck, then knee-strike to the groin.

Fig. 274. Trip the opponent over onto his back …

Fig. 275. ... and apply an Achilles tendon lock.

Fig. 276. Ankle lock.

Fig. 277. Foot lock.

Fig. 278. Toe and ankle lock.

Fig. 279. Knee bar.

Fig. 280. Knee bar with arm wrap.

The Clinch

Standing-up grappling sometimes takes the form of a clinch (see *Jeet Kune Do – A Core Training Manual*). It is important to have a proactive game in the clinch, including strikes with the fist, elbow, knee, head or foot to tenderize an opponent to set up a take-down (see Figs 281–285).

CLOCKWISE FROM TOP LEFT:

Fig. 281. Punching in the clinch.

Fig. 282. Elbow in the clinch.

Fig. 283. Knee in the clinch.

Fig. 284. Head butt in the clinch.

Fig. 285. Foot stomp in the clinch.

Takedowns in the clinch take the form of leg lifts (see Figs 286–290), trips (see Figs 291–294) and hand manipulations like the arm drag (see Figs 295–298),and the arm pop-up (see Figs 299–301).

Fig. 286. From the under and over hook clinch position ...

Fig. 287. ... push the opponent's weight over to your right ...

Fig. 288. ... then step left foot forward.

Fig. 289. Pick up the opponent's left leg with the right hand ...

Fig. 290. ... and take down.

Fig. 291. From the fifty/fifty clinch position ...

Fig. 292. ... scoop your right foot inside the opponent's right leg ...

Fig. 293. ... and backwards with your right foot ...

Fig. 294. ... dropping the opponent to the ground.

Fig. 295. The opponent reaches in to grab your neck.

Fig. 296. Your left forearm wipes the opponent's arm away, as your right hand slides underneath the opponent's arm ...

Fig. 297. ... dragging the opponent's arm across the front of his body.

Fig. 298. Step across with your right leg as you the control opponent's body.

Fig. 299. From the fifty/fifty clinch position ...

Fig. 300. ... pop the opponent's arm up.

Fig. 301. Move in and around to take the opponent's back.

Defending from Your Back

If you end up on your back with an opponent inside your guard (see Figs 302–304),
there are several defensive moves which will
stop an opponent striking you.

Fig. 302. The opponent inside your guard
punches down.

Fig. 303. Snake the opponent's arm and hold
his triceps.

Fig. 304. Hold the opponent's neck and break
his posture.

The first move is to open up your guard, place one foot on the opponent's hip and bring the shin of the other leg across the opponent's chest, using the shin as a defensive shield. This position allows for a scissor sweep that will bring you on top of an opponent in a more favourable position (see Figs 305–307).

Fig. 305. As the opponent tries to pull back to punch, slide your knee across his chest and make a scissors motion with your left leg.

Fig. 306. Transition …

Fig. 307. … to high mount and punch.

The second defensive position is where the knees are brought together in front of an opponent's chest. Putting your feet on his hips will keep him at bay and as he tries to punch-lift up off your hips (see Fig 308).

The third way is the same as the second, but this time the knees must be pointing outwards while controlling the opponent's wrists with your hands (see Fig 309).

The fourth position is to have one of the opponent's arms between your legs as you keep your feet on his hips, while your own hips are raised off the floor (see Fig 310).

Fig. 308. Knees together, hips up.

Fig. 309. Both knees inside, holding the opponent's wrist.

Fig. 310. Keep your feet on the opponent's hips, with one of his arms between your legs.

These four positions can be applied as a defensive shield, but can also be used as a set-up for triangle chokes (see Figs 311–313), arm bars (see Figs 314–318) and escapes while an opponent is on his knees or standing up in your guard (see Figs 319–322).

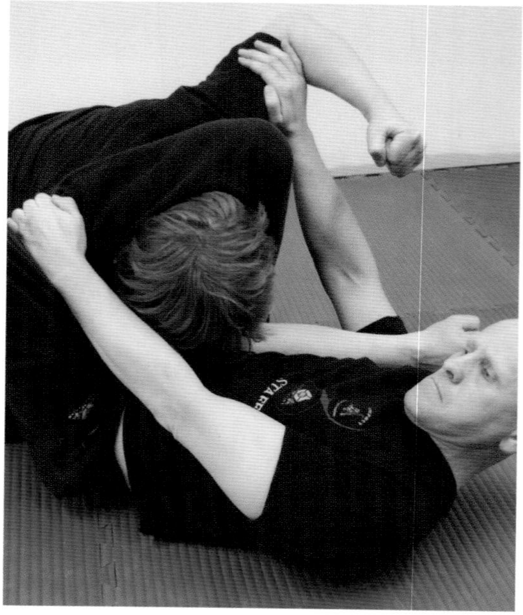

CLOCKWISE FROM TOP LEFT:

Fig. 311. Striking from the open guard.

Fig. 312. Bring your leg over the opponent's shoulder, turn to your side and grab your shin with your left hand.

Fig. 313. Hook your left leg over your right ankle to in order to triangle-choke.

Fig. 314. The opponent punching down from inside your guard.

Fig. 315. Outside parry the opponent's arm across ...

Fig. 316. ... and trap the opponent's arm to your chest.

Fig. 317. Turn on your back and swing your right leg high up on the opponent's back.

CLOCKWISE FROM TOP LEFT:

Fig. 318. Swing your left leg over his left shoulder and raise your hips up to arm bar.

Fig. 319. The opponent stands in your open guard. Keep your feet on his hips.

Fig. 320. As the opponent attempts to punch down, kick upward to his face.

Fig. 321. The opponent falls. Move to defensive shell ...

Fig. 322. ... and stand back up.

The world of grappling techniques is a vast and exciting one in which to become immersed, but be aware that it can take up a considerable amount of training time to become comfortable in uncomfortable positions. From a Jeet Kune Do perspective, the grappling game should be about escape. If training time is limited, then focus on being able to get off your back and onto your feet, or reversing a bad position to a more favourable one that allows you to hit. Also, remember in a street fight situation that ends up on the ground, an opponent may resort to biting, pinching and eye gouging as well as the usual tools of punching, kneeing, elbowing and head-butting. In a street fight anything goes and at some point you might even need to bite your way out.

9 Speed

Probably the first thing anyone remembers about Bruce Lee is his speed. While we may not all be endowed with Lee's fast-twitch muscle-fibre ratio, that is not to say that we cannot improve our own speed. Our genes may have given us a physical limit as to how fast we can become, but if we never train to improve speed it is impossible to know that limit. Fortunately, speed can be broken down into several types and improving one aspect can make up for a lack of ability in another. Speed can be broken down into three areas:

• PERCEPTION (eye)
• COGNITION (brain)
• REACTION (muscle action).

Lee further broke speed down into five types: perceptual speed; mental speed; initiation speed; performance speed; and alteration speed.

Perceptual Speed

Perceptual speed is to do with visual awareness – the quickness of the eye to see openings in an opponent's defence, or to see and recognize approaching attacks. Train yourself to see an opponent's telegraphic motion. Good perceptual speed can help to make up for a slower reaction time or slow performance speed. Make full use of peripheral vision, taking in the whole of the opponent's body and picking up any advancing limb or body movement.

Mental Speed

Mental speed is the speed at which the brain can register and take advantage of what it sees in a split second. In Lee's words: 'I no longer hit, it hits all by itself.' To achieve this, the thought process must become quicker. This only occurs after countless repetitions of correct movement, during which the neurological pathways are developed to make the move spontaneous. Limiting the choice of reactions to a stimulus, be it a kick or a punch, helps to quicken the response. In other words – keep it simple!

Initiation Speed

Initiation speed deals with how fast you can get off the mark, overcoming inertia. This is sometimes known as the 'start speed' and lends itself to 'good form'. For example, the on-guard stance is a 'ready' stance – ready to move in any direction at a split second's notice. The muscles must be in a relaxed state so that when movement is necessary, the body can move quickly without tension. However, a state of readiness, or muscle tone, must be maintained while in the bai-jong so that muscular contraction can occur in an instant.

Performance Speed

Performance speed is the type of speed that comes to mind when you watch a fast punch or kick – how fast it travels from point A to

B. The amount of tension in the antagonistic muscle can be the deciding factor in the delivery speed of an attack. The antagonists are the opposing muscle group to the agonist or prime mover – for example, the prime mover for straightening the elbow is the triceps muscle, therefore the antagonistic muscle would be the biceps muscle. In order for the elbow to straighten or extend properly, the bicep must be able to relax enough to allow this movement with less risk of injury. Too much tension in the antagonistic muscles impedes performance.

Alteration Speed

Alteration speed is the ability to change direction mid-flow. To do this quickly requires a high level of co-ordination, balance and footwork.

Being aware of these five types of speed can help you to discover your own strengths and weaknesses in this vital attribute, thus helping you to train to your maximum potential.

10 Countering Hand Immobilization Attack

Bruce Lee listed 'hand immobilization attack' as one of the 'five ways of attack'. Most Jeet Kune Do practitioners become skilful in the art of hand immobilization and a considerable amount of training time is given to the development of 'tactile awareness' – the ability to feel an opponent's intentions through the sense of touch. This attribute is developed to a high degree through specific exercises like chi-sau or sticking hands (see Jeet Kune Do – A Core Structure Training Manual). Chi-sau makes you very sensitive to the movement and energy of a training partner's arms and helps to speed up contact reflex and reaction time when you have a connection with an opponent's limbs.

Trapping is used to remove barriers that are put in the way of strikes, be it a parry or block, or can be used to control an opponent's lead arm on entry so as to avoid a stop-hit.

Most trapping techniques require some kind of structure to work against, which is why hand immobilization attacks work well against opponents who favour blocking first before counter-attacking. The block or parry first can leave the limb susceptible to a trap.

The first line of defence against a trapper is to give him no set structure to attach to. By making small movements and keeping your lead hand elusive, an opponent will be unable to gain an attachment in order to immobilize the arm. Using this approach gives the opponent no set line to enter with a simultaneous pak-sau chung-chuie punch. As an opponent push-shuffles in an attempt to trap your lead hand and thereby avoid your stop-hit counter, simply retract your lead hand back along the runway (an imaginary line running from the hip to an opponent's chin, on which the lead forearm rests). Avoiding an opponent's pak-sau, immediately return fire with a lead straight punch. I like to call this a 'trigger punch' (see Figs 323–325).

Fig. 323. On guard facing an opponent.

Fig. 324. Opponent moves in to trap and hit.

Fig. 325. Slide lead hand back and trigger-punch in the open line.

If the opponent makes contact with his pak-sau, then various forms of counter-trapping and disengagements can be used.

Counter pak-sau chung-chuie with:
• Pak-sau chung-chuie (counter the trap with a trap) (see Figs 326–328).

CLOCKWISE FROM TOP LEFT:

Fig. 326. On guard.

Fig. 327. Opponent feeds a pak-sau chung-chuie.

Fig. 328. Counter his trap with a trap of your own.

• Jau-sau, running hand, (disengagement) (see Figs 329–331 below).

CLOCKWISE FROM TOP LEFT:

Fig. 329. On guard.

Fig. 330. Opponent feeds a pak-sau chung-chuie.

Fig. 331. Counter with a disengagement.

• Outside sliding lever – bridge punch   (see Figs 332–334 below).

Fig. 332. On
guard.

Fig. 333.
Opponent feeds a
pak-sau chung-
chuie.

Fig. 334. Counter
with outside
sliding lever.

• Inside sliding lever, biu-jee (see Figs 335–336).

If the opponent successfully traps your lead hand and fires a chung-chuie which you parry with the rear hand, he will then attempt to clear your rear-hand barrier with a second hand immobilization. If you have a well-trained sense of tactile awareness you can counter in the midst of his second trap (see Figs 337–340).

Remember the closer you move towards an opponent the more you will lose visual reaction time and so the highly developed tactile awareness should take over. When there is contact with an opponent's limbs you no longer need to see where an opponent's hands are, you simply 'feel' and control his movement.

Fig. 335. On guard.

Fig. 336. Opponent feeds a pak-sau chung-chuie. Counter with inside sliding lever.

Fig. 337. On guard.

Fig. 338. Opponent feeds a pak-sau chung chuie.

Fig. 339. Opponent attempts to lop-sau the rear barrier. Start to slide your lead hand under ...

Fig. 340. ... checking behind the opponent's elbow, plus a rear chung-chuie.

11   Focus Glove Training

Dan Inosanto was responsible for introducing Bruce Lee to most of the training equipment that is used in Jeet Kune Do. The focus gloves appeared around 1964. This idea was taken from British boxers but used in a unique way that involved not only punching, but also trapping, kicking, elbowing and kneeing. Lee, together with Inosanto, created many drills to cover all ranges and tools in attack and defence. Lee used the focus glove extensively in Hong Kong prior to his death.

The focus glove is probably the most useful training device in Jeet Kune Do. Almost every offensive tool can be trained on the gloves. At its highest level, focus-glove training can be the closest thing to sparring, but like most things in Jeet Kune Do there is a training progression.

Beginners

In this first stage the student learns how to stand and position the pads for the various basic tools. This is an important stage, as the pad man learns to settle in and gets used to feeling the impact of the punches. On the other hand, the student feeding the punches starts with single tool development, working on economy of motion and good form. Speed and power come later. The pad holder helps to correct his partner's form, checking that his elbows stay in on straight shots and that the guarding hand remains up at all times. If the trainee drops his guard or leaves a line uncovered, the trainer can fire a light shot with the focus pad into the open line to help the student take care of his defence.

Another great exercise in the early stages of development is to move the focus gloves to train a student's reaction time. The pad man holds the gloves together in front of his chest – this is known as the prayer position (see Fig 341).

Fig. 341. The prayer position.

The pad man then flashes a single pad in one of the single tool positions. The student training his visual awareness learns to read the line of attack presented by the pad man and quickly returns the corresponding attack (see Figs 342–360).

Fig. 342. Pad man in prayer position with trainee.

Fig. 343. Flashes pad for jab or lead straight.

Fig. 344. Lead straight.

Fig. 345. Flashes pad for rear straight.

141

Fig. 346. Rear straight.

Fig. 347. Flashes pad for lead hook.

Fig. 348. Lead hook.

Fig. 349. Flashes pad for rear uppercut.

Fig. 350. Rear uppercut.

Fig. 351. Flashes pad for lead uppercut.

Fig. 352. Lead uppercut.

Fig. 353. Flashes pad for rear overhead.

Fig. 354. Rear overhead.

Fig. 355. Flashes pad for rear hook.

Fig. 356. Rear hook.

Fig. 357. Flashes pad for lead body hook.

Fig. 358. Lead body hook.

Fig. 359. Flashes pad for rear body hook.

Fig. 360. Rear body hook.

Intermediate

By now, the pad man should be able to feed the focus pads in the correct position and set the pads for a number of combinations. Both the trainee and trainer can start to move around more freely using distance and footwork. The pad man can now call out the combination and the trainer answers back with the correct combination of strikes. The pad man also hit

Fig. 361. Pad man feeds rear overhead; defend with lead forearm cover ...

Fig. 362. ... to rear uppercut.

Fig. 363. Lead hook.

Fig. 364. Rear straight.

ack to make sure his training partner is always aking care of his defence.

At this stage, the holder can now attack long specific lines with various tools that force the trainee to develop specific defences to the attack, then follow up with the most natural and realistic combination of strikes (see Figs 361–364 and 365–368).

Fig. 365. Pad man lead jabs to body; counter with rear elbow tuck ...

Fig. 366. ... to lead uppercut.

Fig. 367. Rear straight.

Fig. 368. Lead hook.

Advanced

Advanced focus glove training should allow the trainee to develop and use the five ways of attack and the four-corner defences (see Jeet Kune Do – A Core Structure Training Manual). Also, a variety of combinations of hands and feet to the high, middle and low lines of attack are developed. A blend of kicking, punching, trapping and clinch work should be covered, along with the use of broken rhythm. Remember, this should be the next best thing to sparring (see Figs 369–376).

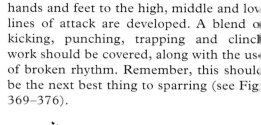

Fig. 369. Lead jab.

Fig. 370. Pad man feeds rear straight; counter slip inside ...

Fig. 371. ... to lead hook.

Fig. 372. Rear straight.

Fig. 373. Pad man feeds lead round kick; counter with cut kick.

Fig. 374. Step forward and rear straight.

Fig. 375. Lead hook.

376. Fig. 376. Rear straight.

Focus Pad Progression

First Step – Basic isolation of single tools.
Second Step – Focus pad positions (reaction time).
Third Step – Combinations of two, three and four count. Following are examples of these combinations:

Two-count examples:

• jab – rear straight
• jab – rear uppercut
• jab – rear overhead
• jab – rear hook
• double jab
• jab – lead hook
• high jab – low jab
• low jab – high jab
• low jab – rear straight
• rear straight – lead hook
• rear straight – lead uppercut
• rear straight – rear uppercut
• rear straight – rear overhead
• lead hook – rear straight
• lead hook – rear uppercut
• lead hook – rear overhead
• lead uppercut – rear straight
• lead uppercut – rear overhead
• lead uppercut – rear hook
• lead uppercut – lead hook
• rear uppercut – lead hook
• rear uppercut – rear overhead.

Three-count examples:

• jab – rear straight – hook
• jab – rear uppercut – hook
• jab – rear overhead – lead uppercut
• jab – rear straight to body – lead uppercut
• jab – rear straight to body – lead hook
• jab – rear straight – lead body hook
• rear straight – lead hook – rear straight
• rear straight – lead uppercut – rear straight
• rear straight – lead uppercut – lead hook
• rear straight – lead uppercut – rear hook
• rear straight – lead uppercut – rear overhead

• lead uppercut – rear straight – lead hook
• lead uppercut – rear overhead – lead uppercut
• lead uppercut – rear hook – lead hook
• lead uppercut – lead hook – rear straight
• lead uppercut – lead hook – rear overhead
• rear uppercut – lead hook – rear straight
• rear uppercut – lead hook – rear overhead
• rear overhead – lead uppercut – rear overhead
• rear overhead – lead uppercut – rear straight
• rear overhead – lead hook – rear uppercut.

Four-count examples (with broken rhythm):

• jab – rear straight – lead hook – rear straight
• jab – rear straight– lead hook – rear overhead
• jab – rear straight – lead hook – rear uppercut
• rear straight – lead hook – rear straight – lead uppercut
• rear straight – lead hook – rear straight – lead hook
• rear straight – lead uppercut – rear straight – lead hook
• lead hook – rear straight – lead uppercut – rear straight
• lead hook – rear uppercut – lead hook – rear straight
• lead hook – rear overhead – lead uppercut – rear straight
• rear hook – lead uppercut – rear straight – lead hook
• rear hook – lead hook – rear uppercut – lead hook
• rear overhead – lead uppercut – rear straight – lead hook
• rear overhead – lead hook – rear straight – lead uppercut.

Fourth Step – Pad holder attacks specific lines – defend and counter.
Fifth Step – Advanced drills – five ways of attack, broken rhythm, four-corner defence, clinch.

12 Sparring

Sparring in Jeet Kune Do is applying what you have learnt against a live, resisting opponent; it is not a real fight. There are restrictions on certain tools, such as finger jabs to the eyes and strikes to the groin and knee – these attacks are left out for the obvious safety of the fighters. Sparring allows you to apply the body of techniques in a more realistic situation.

There are numerous benefits to sparring. Learning to hit a moving, uncooperative target requires great accuracy, timing and judgment of distance and being able to keep composure while under pressure can only be learnt from sparring 'fight time'. Taking a hard blow can be really unnerving and difficult to accept and in the early stages it is easy to become angry and upset, wanting to retaliate with an even harder blow, resulting in a brawl that defeats the object of sparring. Remember, sparring should be a learning experience, analysing why, for instance, you got hit in order to improve on any weakness in your defence. Learning can only take place if you remain calm. Anger stunts growth.

Before sparring, a great deal of time must be given towards mastering the basic fundamental techniques of Jeet Kune Do. During sparring, or fighting for that matter, you cannot afford to be thinking about the technique and strategies that you need to employ. These should be engraved into the subconscious so that the mind can be free to focus on an opponent. The mind and body must be trained on a regular basis and with much repetition in order for the correct response to come automatically to the surface. This training helps you to function freely while sparring. Bruce Lee referred to this as 'learn – abide – dissolve'. First, learn a technique and understand the correct mechanics and form. Secondly, 'abide' or stick with the technique – this takes hours and hours of drilling. Thirdly, to 'dissolve' the technique is to embed it into the subconscious mind and make it your own.

In Jeet Kune Do, there is progression in sparring. The three stages are cooperative, semi-cooperative and uncooperative.

Cooperative Sparring

To begin with, the Jeet Kune Do practitioner should start with simple cooperative drilling. Here are some examples:

• Opponent A feeds a jab, opponent B parries the jab with his rear hand, then returns a jab, opponent A parries the jab (see Figs 377–380).

Fig. 377. On guard.

Fig. 378. Opponent feeds jab; counter with rear-hand parry.

Fig. 379. Return a jab; opponent rear-hand parry.

Fig. 380. Opponent returns a second jab; counter with rear-hand parry.

• Opponent A feeds a jab rear straight. Opponent B catches the jab, then shoulder-rolls away from the rear straight.

Opponent B returns fire with a rear straight. Opponent A shoulder-rolls with a simultaneous side kick (see Figs 381–384).

Fig. 381. On guard.

Fig. 382. Jab countered with a rear parry.

Fig. 383. Rear straight countered with a shoulder roll.

Fig. 384. Return with a rear straight, countered with a simultaneous shoulder roll plus side kick.

Fig. 385. Shoulder roll.

Fig. 386. Wing-arm deflection.

Fig. 387. Slip outside with lead uppercut.

Fig. 388. Slip outside with rear straight to body.

Fig. 389. Students in the midst of sparring.

Fig. 390. Live sparring.

It is important at this early stage of drilling for a student to be brought on carefully and with purpose. He should start off slowly and learn to read the lines of attack. As the student gains confidence and learns to keep his eyes open at all times, the speed of the drill can then increase to real time.

Semi-cooperative Sparring

These drills are part-set, but with an open-ended finish. This means that the first few moves are pre-arranged, while the final move is freelance, making the fighter cover, parry or counter-attack.

Here is an example:

• Using the same drill as the co-operative exercise, opponent A reacts to opponent B's return differently each time (see Figs 385–388).

Uncooperative Sparring

This is the closest thing to a real fight. The fighters are now encouraged to use a full range of tools as they try to outmanoeuvre each other, trying to hit without getting hit and eventually moving up to full speed. Both fighters can agree beforehand on the level of power they wish to use; in sparring, this is known as fighting without the 'bite of the intent to hurt' (see Figs 389–390).

Different Scenarios

Different skills can be developed in sparring rounds. The teacher may set the round so that certain tools are developed. For example, the round could be:

• lead hand versus lead hand
• lead hand versus both hands
• lead hand versus lead hand and lead foot
• lead hand and lead foot versus lead hand and lead foot
• lead hand versus lead foot
• lead hand and foot versus both hands
• both hands versus both hands.

In all sparring the safety of the fighters must be paramount, making sure that both parties are wearing proper protective gear, which would include mouthpiece, gloves and groin guard. Baseball shin guards must be used if stop-kicks are allowed.

Appendix:
Fencing Terminology Used in Jeet Kune Do

absence of blade when the blades are not touching; non-attachment.

advance moving forward.

attack any offensive movement used to strike an opponent.

attack on preparation to stop-hit on an opponent's preparation to attack.

attack on the blade the preparation for an attack (e.g., beat pressure).

beat the preparation of attack against an opponent's blade, to open a line or to gain a reaction.

bind the preparation of attack that takes an opponent's blade from high to low line diagonally.

breaking ground retreating footwork.

broken time a pause during a combination attack.

cadence the rhythm of movements.

change of engagements changing from one engagement to another in a new line.

circular parry circling an opponent's blade; sometimes called a 'counter-parry'.

close quarters close-range fighting.

compound attack an attack that starts with a feint.

counter-time second intention; any action made against an opponent's attempt to stop-hit.

croisé the preparation of attack taking the blade from the high to low line on the same side of engagement.

derobement evading an opponent's attempt to beat on the blade.

detachment parry a parry that does not stick to an opponent's blade.

disengagement changing the blade from the line of engagement to the opposite line by passing under an opponent's blade.

engagement the crossing of the blades.

envelopment a circle motion on opponent's blade returning to original line of engagement without loss of contact.

evasion see 'derobement'.

false attack an attack that is not intended to land on an opponent.

feint an offensive movement made to look like an attack in order to draw a reaction from an opponent.

fencing measure the distance between two opponents.

fencing time the time taken to execute one movement.

fleche a method of delivering the running attack.

gaining ground moving forward.

gaining on the lunge stepping the rear foot up close to the lead foot before lunging.

high lines visible targets above the sword hand when on guard.

indirect a simple attack made in another line.

inside lines targets inside of the blade arm.

invitations opening a line of attack.

low lines targets visible below the blade arm.
lunge extension of the blade arm combined with footwork.

on guard the ready position.
opposition a parry that sticks to an opponent's blade.

parry a defensive move used to deflect an opponent's blade.
pied ferme a movement made without footwork.
pressure the preparation of attack made by pressing on an opponent's blade to gain a reaction.
prise de fer the taking of an opponent's blade (e.g., engagement, bind, croisé and envelopment).
progressive attack a compound attack, continuously moving towards the target while cutting time and distance to a minimum.

recovery returning to the on-guard position.
redoublement a renewal of attack while on the lunge.
remise while on the lunge, replacing the point of the blade on the same target without withdrawing the blade.
renewed attack remise, redoublement or reprise.
reprise the renewal of attack after momentarily returning to on guard.
riposte an offensive attack after making a parry.

second intention an offensive attack made after an opponent has been forced to make a stop-hit.
semicircular parry a parry that moves through a semicircular movement from high to low, or
low to high.
sentiment du fer feeling an opponent's reactions through contact with his blade.
simple attack an attack with one blade movement that can be direct or indirect.
stance the correct on-guard position.
stop-hit a counter-attack; an attack into an opponent's attack.

taking the blade preparation of attack (*see* prise de fer).
timing fencing movements made at the correct moment.

Index